2020

Robert robinson

from

Mick Murphy (fan)

November 1976.

ORDINARY LIVES

edited by

CLIVE MURPHY

I stared with the crowds at Mrs Ali while she smashed milk bottles, directed traffic, and sang and danced and shouted in the roadway. But how did we appear to her? How did she appear to herself? I asked her to stare back . . . This, her autobiography, is the first of a series of portraits dedicated against 'the man on the Clapham omnibus'—if he exists.

EDITOR

THE GOOD DEEDS OF A GOOD WOMAN

Beatrice Ali

THE GOOD DEEDS
OF A GOOD WOMAN

Recorded between May and September 1975

LONDON : DENNIS DOBSON

First published in Great Britain 1976 by
Dobson Books Ltd, 80 Kensington Church Street, London, W8

Printed in Great Britain by
Bristol Typesetting Co, Ltd,
Barton Manor, St Philips, Bristol

ISBN 0 234 77891 1

To
Michael and Derek

ONE

When my husband run away from me to East Pakistan everybody was shouting, 'Oh your Basit's married!', 'Basit's got
another wife now!', 'Basit won't want you any more!' They
used to stand on one side of the road, and I was on the other walking down. 'What are you going to do now, Mrs Ali!', 'What
are you going to do?!', 'She's a young girl. You're old!' I said,
'Please don't make trouble! What is done is done. Let bygones
be bygones. I don't want to hear any more about him. Please!
Wherever he may be and whatever he's doing, let him do it!'
They was criticizing me: 'How are you going to live? Are you
going on the streets?' I said, 'For God's sake no! What are my
hands made for?!! I've worked since I was nine. I've been
brought up the hard way!' They said, 'What do you mean "the
hard way"?' I said, 'To use my hands and not my body!'

Basit's relations, even, didn't want to know me. When we was
married they used to come to dinner, but as soon as he run away
everything was finished. They said, 'Why after all these years,
Beatty?' I said, 'He wanted to go back to his own country and
get married. It was his idea.' But they classed me as no good. I
turned round and said, 'Well I couldn't have been so bad for
him to stay with me for thirty years!'

There come a time later when I'd moved into the Salvation
Army Hostel, Hopetown Street, and I was going out one day
to do a job for someone and I met a person and he said, 'Oh
your Basit's dead now.' Another two come along. 'Oh dead now.
Husband.' I said, 'Leave me *alone*. Sod off!', and I'm making
my way nearer and nearer to the place where I'm going and
another two come along and *they* started and I called them
names. I said, 'You're only rubbish! Khobbis! To hell with
you! And to hell with him for what he done to me!'

A*   9

I didn't believe them. But when I was on my way back to the Salvation Army Hostel one night I saw a man in Brick Lane I hadn't seen for twenty years and I called him, I said, 'Formas! Formas!' He said, 'Oh my God! Beatty, I've been looking for you!' I said, 'How's Basit getting on?' He said, 'To tell you the truth, Booh-by,' he said, 'I feel very sorry but Basit has been dead five months.' I said, 'Are you sure, Formas?' He said, 'I'm sure. I'm positive.' I said, 'Are you telling me the truth? I've heard he's dead so many times but I don't want no lies!' He said, 'Basit has been dead five months.' I said, 'On your life this is the truth?' He said, 'Yes. Ami bhalo mat. He was against the Bangladesh and he died doing three years in prison.'

So I went to see my son, Michael. I told him he'd lost his Dad. He said, 'Forget about it, Mum. Don't think about it. Think what's going to happen. Look for your future. Enjoy yourself!' And I did, I went to the E.1. Festival on Bigland Grass. I said to a young girl with a lovely expression, 'Come on! We'll have this dance!' Jiving. Let's twist again! Let your body shake rattle and roll! We danced so much I wore my soles out. They was taking our photo. I went on stage, I asked, 'Can I sing a song I've made up?' but the man said, 'Very sorry. Maybe some other time.'

'Oh my Momma and Papa have gone from me for evermore.
Oh my Momma and Papa I'll always remember you by the
song you sang
When I was a baby on your knee.
But the time has come for me to think of my future
Now that you've gone from me for evermore.
Oh my Momma and Papa have gone from me for evermore
But your memory stays with me for evermore.
And my sisters and brother have gone from me for evermore.
But there'll come a time when we'll meet again sometime
If it's only on the corner of the street.
La la la la. La la la la.
Oh my Momma and Papa and my sisters and brother have
gone from me for evermore.'

My mother before she died in 1947 she looked at me, she looked at my two sisters and my brother, she said, 'Beatty and

Minnie and Dorothy and Derek, I'm going into the New World. If anybody needs any help, please help them. Never say No. What you do for people will be paid back in another way.' She smiled and that was the finish.

So though I'm a pensioner myself I buy second hand curtains in Cheshire Street Market, I go to the washing machine, I wash them out, I look around, I knock on doors of old people. 'Want some curtains, love? Want me to clean your windows? I don't want no money. You're like my second Mum.' They say, 'All right. You come. You do.' I do. There's old people I've known in Old Nichol Street and they say, 'Beatty, come up and have a cup of tea!', and if the place is dirty I get hot water and I do the place out. If I'd a lot of money I'd look for the old people. I'd invite about a hundred and fifty on a charabanc outing to Brighton or Margate and then come back and provide them with a tea.

I've been doing good deeds all my life and whatever I've done I've done it with a good heart. I reckon I deserve a gold medal. If I see an old lady who wants to go across the road I even do that. I saved an old lady's life six months ago, a blind lady at the corner of Vallance Road. She was walking across the road with a white stick. I see a car coming full speed wanting to jump the lights. Quick! I run into the middle of the road and pulled her back onto the pavement. She's asking me, 'Why did you pull me back, love?' I said, 'To save your life. I've lost my mother but you are my second mother. If I hadn't brought you back onto the pavement a car would have been bang on. When I look and see you my mind says, "That's my second Mum. What can I do?"' She was eighty-six. I stood still with her for half an hour to steady her down. I say 'Where do you live?' She says, 'In Philchurch Street.' I say, 'All right, Mum, I take you where you live.' Three flights of stairs I took her. She opened the flat I stayed with her for two hours. We had a cup of tea. She said, 'Who you are I cannot see because I am blind, but thank you very much.' I said, 'Don't worry, Mum. God will look for you. God bless you. I hope to see you again. Goodbye. You all right, Mum?' 'Yes, I'm all right.'

I've been brought up good. If anybody needs help I help that person. Ama cushi, toma cushi. If I help a person I say, 'Thank

God I've helped that person today. Maybe I might need help from them one day.' I knew a woman for twenty-five years. There come a time when I went to her door. Seven flights of stairs. She said, 'Go away from my door! I don't want to see you no more!' I never see that woman for one year, but then she needed me. I'd to run for Dr Wallis. Dr Wallis came. 'But for you,' he said, 'she would have been underneath. Mrs Ali, you're a brick. Her temperature was a hundred and three.' I said to Dr Wallis, 'Look, I knew Cathy for twenty-five years, but there's been a year since she sent me away from her door. Maybe there'll come a time when I might need her more than she might need me, but this time she needed me more than I needed her.' You always find that. You've got a good friend and you have trouble with that friend and there comes a time when that friend needs you.

I used to help Georgina in her coffee shop in Brick Lane to occupy my mind. One day somebody come in and said, 'I'd like to hear that song of yours that you sung last week.' I sung it. Georgina got hold of me and chucked me out. Another day I was in there and I sung it and a great big stout woman picked up a sauce bottle and aimed it at my head. She said, 'You must be fucking mad!' I said, 'To hell with you!' and Georgina chucked me out again.

But I've got a good friend in Back Church Lane Post Office. When you go in there he's always smiling and waving. He seen me with some plants one day. 'What!' he said. 'Are they for me?!' So I said, 'You like plants?' He said, 'Yes.' 'All right,' I said, 'you can have them if you like,' and I handed them over to him. He never forgot about that. I went in there one Thursday morning. I said, 'Would you like me to buy you a cigar or some cigarettes?' He said, 'I don't smoke, love.' So I went out and I bought bread pudding and egg and tomato rolls and cheese rolls for him and the whole of the people that was sitting at the counter. I spent nearly a pound. I handed them over. He said, 'You shouldn't have done that. You can't afford it.' I said, 'You're such a nice chap, I done it with a good heart.' He's an Indian. He isn't very old. I should say he was around forty-five, not more than forty-eight. He's got such a lovely face. There's good people and there's bad people amongst coloureds.

I treat all people like a sister. One day I was sitting on a seat in Waterloo Station. An old lady came and sit next to me, smoking a cigarette. I had another look. I seem to know that face from somewhere. We get talking. She says, 'Whereabouts did you come from, love? You don't mind my asking?' 'I come from Luton,' I said. 'Well,' she said, 'that's a funny thing,' she said. 'I was born and bred in Luton.' So she said to me, 'What street did you live in?' I said, '51, Windsor Street.' 'By gee,' she said, 'that's funny! I only lived round the corner!' She said, 'Your mother's name was Mrs Webster, wasn't it?' I said, 'Yes.' 'Ooh!' she said. 'We were neighbours!'

She had a lovely complexion and no make-up, and she was making herself a skirt. I said to her, 'Excuse me, love, but how old are you?' How old do you think she was? Eighty-six! I said, 'Eighty-six!' I said, 'No, Mum, you're not eighty-six!' 'I am, you know, love. Look! Here's my birth certificate.' So I said to her, 'Whereabouts do you live, love?' She said, 'In Waterloo Road Hostel. We have to come out in the morning time but we can go back four o'clock. But I don't go back four o'clock, love,' she said. 'I go back ten o'clock.' So she looked at me, she said, 'What time do *you* have to be in, then?' 'Well,' I said, 'at half past ten.' So we asked somebody the time. I said, 'Excuse me, mister, could you tell us the right time?' He said, 'It's eight o'clock, love.' So I said to this lady, I said, 'Come, Mum, I'll buy you a coffee and I'll buy you a sandwich and then we'll have a smoke and I'll see you to your door, and then I'm going back to the Salvation Army Hostel, Hopetown Street.' She said, 'I think you're very nice, Beatty. We'll meet again some time, won't we? Can I see you again?' I said, 'Yes.' So she said to me, 'How about making it next Thursday?' I said, 'All right, Mum. I'll see you next Thursday.' She said, 'What time?' I said, 'Four o'clock, love.'

So I'm getting ready in the hostel. I looked at the time. It's two o'clock. I caught the bus to Waterloo Station. There she was, bless her. She said, 'Oh hello, Beatty! You did keep your promise,' she said. 'I thought you would never come.' I said, 'If I promise to meet someone, I meet them. We can go now, Mum, and have dinner in the snack bar. I've got money today, love. Come. What do you want? What do you fancy?' She said,

'Anything, Beatty.' I said, 'Would you like sausages and chips and tomatoes?' 'Oh yes!' 'Two slices?' 'Oh yes!' 'Coffee?' 'No. Cup of tea, Beatty.' So we enjoyed that, we had a smoke, we had a walk round, we sat on a seat, we spoke to each other. Then she looked at the clock, she said, 'Come, Beatty. The time's getting on, love. It's nine o'clock and I've to be in at ten.' So we hurried along and I left her at the door. 'Good night, Nan. See you again soon.'

Two weeks later I'm in Brick Lane Market and she's coming along. 'Ooh!' I said. 'Hello!' 'Hello, Beatty!' I said, 'Cup of tea today, Nan?' 'Yes,' she said. 'Cake?' 'Yes.' So we go in a coffee shop. Cake each. Tea each. Cigarette each. 'Another cup of tea, Nan?' 'Yes, another cup of tea.' 'Right.' Then she says, 'I've promised to see someone at five o'clock. You don't mind, do you, Beatty?' 'No, love. See you again soon.'

I'm a fool when I've got money. My heart is very soft. I'd give to anybody. About four months ago I was walking through Fieldgate Street and in Fieldgate Street there's a butcher's shop, and I saw an old man with two sticks and he's looking at these lamb chops. 'Oh they're lovely big meaty chops!' He looked at me. 'Oh Mum,' he said, 'I wouldn't half love four chops! Two for me and two for my wife!' I had money. I went in. I said, 'Four of them nice meaty chops, love!' How much do you think they were? A pound! I said to the old man, 'They're only a pound, love.' He said, 'You're not buying them for *me,* surely?!' I said, 'Yes,' and I bought him a tin of peas as well. And, funny thing, I was lucky that day. If you help anybody, you're often lucky. I went into the betting office and I won £10 on the horses. And I was lucky another day and all. All I had on me was thirty pence and I was sitting looking at the paper. 'I don't know, I think I'll have a bet today.' So I went into the betting office, looked at the names of the dogs and had a toss-up. 'Shall I do 1 and 3 or 2 and 3 or 1 and 5? 1 and 5.' Twenty-eight pence forecast. Bet on. Out. Went for a walk right down Mile End. Had my dinner in a coffee shop, and afterwards a coffee and a smoke. Come out. Slowly walk back to the betting office. Guvnor's looking at me. 'You're smiling today, ain't you? You don't know how much you've won, do you?' I said, 'No.' He said, 'You've won £35.'

I want my book to be called 'The Good Deeds of a Good Woman'. I stuck to my man for thirty years and during all them years I helped people. People come to my home who had no money and I kept them in food and cigarettes and went out of my way to find them a job. One night we seen a boy about nineteen that come from India, and he come to live with us for one year. I looked for him till my husband got him a job at £15 a week, and he worked his way up, he got £25. Then he come up till he got £35 and now this same boy is earning nearly £50 a week. Maybe the book should be called 'A Good Wife of Many Good Deeds' or 'I'm the Good Girl that Likes People of Many Countries' or 'A Good Wife that Loves People from All Over the World'. When there was the flood in East Pakistan I appeared in a drama at Toynbee Hall, Commercial Street. I danced to Bangladesh records and I brought apples and bananas and pan for selling. There was a young Bangladesh boy come from the West End dressed up as a Bangladesh girl with a sari on and a black wig. He danced among the crowd. Someone else had to pretend to be a doctor. We collected £144.

I walk around helping everybody I can. I even helped Elsie. I come to meet her in Brick Lane. She was sitting on a step near Georgina's. She looked at me, she said, 'Hello, Mrs! I'm dying for a smoke.' I said, 'All right, love, here you are, there's four cigarettes. And here you are, there's two shillings to go and have a cup of tea.' And then I met her again in Commercial Street near the coffee stall. That time she had no money either. She said, 'Can you buy me a cup of tea?' I said, 'Do you want anything to eat as well?' She said, 'Yes, a meat pie.' That was thirty pence. Then she asked me for cigarettes. I gave her four cigarettes.

Another day I was walking down Brick Lane and coming towards Princelet Street, the laundriette on the corner. I saw Elsie. She was all made up. She looked very nice. I said, 'Elsie, love, where are you going?' She said, 'I'm going to see my children, Beatty.' I said, 'How many children have you got, then?' 'Oh,' she said, 'six,' and she showed me their photos. Lovely children. So I said, 'How did you come to part from your husband?' 'Well,' she said, 'it's a long story, Beatty. I wouldn't like to tell you. My husband was a man with money,

15

a gypsy. The trouble is,' she said, 'he's got another woman. But I'm allowed to go and see the children every now and again.'

She wanted a skirt made but the material she bought was a bit grubby. So I was thinking to myself, 'Well, Elsie's a nice girl. She's like my own daughter.' I asked her, 'What waist are you, Elsie?' She said, 'Twenty-eight.' So I took a walk over to Wentworth Street and I picked up a nice grey skirt on a stall there with a flare and a flare and a flare—ten shillings—and I took her in Bethnal Green Road toilets and she had a wash, did her hair, and she put on the skirt. She said, 'I want a blouse.' I said, 'Hang on! I'll run to the hostel. I've got a white blouse I'll give you.' So she put the white blouse on. 'Oh,' she said, 'don't I look nice, Beatty?! Thank God you give me these!'

She's only forty. She's been sleeping down on Euston Station lately, but she's come away from there. I saw her this morning. She looked pretty rough—all in. She's got terrible legs, bless her. Varicose veins. She's an unlucky woman. One night when it was bitter cold she was sleeping by the great big fire in Spitalfields Market and all of a sudden she rolled over and come right on top of the fire. She burned her legs in the front from the knee to the ankle and all her hands was all burnt and the skin was coming off. But she's a pretty girl when she's made up, and she's got lovely hair. And she's all right so long as you're giving her —buying her a cup of tea, buying her something to eat and cigarettes. But maybe come a time when you can't afford it, and then she don't like it and she'll turn on you, she'll tell you to eff off.

They wouldn't have her in the Salvation Army Hostel. She come there two or three times and the Major said, 'I'm sorry, Elsie, you can't.' She does a bit of the other, and if you're sleeping in a doorway night after night, night after night, and you don't have a bath, you're bound to be running alive. You could pick them things up anywhere. She could bring in lice and we'd all have to go to the Cleansing Station. You've got to be very, very careful. That's why I have a good wash down every morning and every night I go in the bath.

People say to me, 'Blimey! Got another new thing today?! Where are you getting your clothes?!' I say, 'I buy them. They're not new. They're second hand.' I go to the Oxfam shop,

Vallance Road. She knows my size. Suits fifteen pence, ten pence a blouse, ten pence a skirt—she's loaded up with stuff in there. She goes down Cheshire Street Market and picks up odds and ends. I was in there the other day. You ought to have seen the lovely clothes a nurse from the London Hospital give her! Shoes and a lovely coat and a lovely blue dress with a belt and sequins. A great armful she brought in! Then there's Harry Fishman in the paper shop. He's got a heart of gold that man. Any time you go in there with a couple of coupons, 'Here you are, a packet of cigarettes. Here you are, a box of matches.' He's been in the shop for years and years. In his younger days he was a policeman. I went in there one day. 'Here you are, Beatty. Here's a couple of pairs of tights.' Another day I went in. 'Here you are'—a lovely red dress and a skirt.

There's an old lady in the room next to me in the hostel. I should say she must be over eighty. She wears great big men's boots that's cut down. She's got a jumper on that's got safety-pins and safety-pins and safety-pins. She's got trousers that's pinned and pinned and pinned and pinned and pinned till you can't pin them no more. No need for it.

There's nine people in my bedroom. Nine people! Some you can get on with, some you can't. One woman don't buy no clothes at all. All she's got is what she stands up in. She takes off this dark blue mack, shakes it and rolls it up with her skirt, puts it in a bag and gets into the bed in her jumper and covers herself over. Then, the next morning, the same jumper, the same skirt, the same mack. That mack she's got, well you wouldn't put it in the dustbin it's so broken. Yet every night she strips the bed off, shakes the blankets and shakes the sheets and turns over the mattress and sprays it with Keatings Powder. That goes on for half an hour. Then she'll spray the room with air-freshener. And she's got a habit with flies. She says, 'You bastard! Go away! Leave me alone!' and grabs at them. She gets on my nerves. She won't let you speak after nine. Every week she goes and has one of them sauna baths. Why spend money for that when she could go and rig herself out? Why buy camphor balls? Why buy things you stand and hang in the lavatory for smells? She can't understand why she can't get a job. She thinks everybody's against her. One evening she was saying to someone while

I was smoking a cigarette, 'I cannot understand why I cannot find a job.' I butted in, I said, 'Maybe it's because you're not dressed properly. If you're going for a job with a torn mack and torn shoes, naturally the Guvnor's going to weigh you up and down. It's the condition,' I said, 'you're going *after* the jobs. Your *mind* should tell you that. It must be you look clean and respectable to go and get a job. You've got to look *clean*. It could be the sort of job where you've got to be examined,' I said. 'I've been in jobs where I've had to go upstairs and be examined from top to bottom, and I can honestly say that I've got good references as a result. I've worked in a Kardomah Coffee Bar. I've worked in Shell Mex. I've worked in the Oran Oil Company.' She said, 'To hell with you! Mind your own business!' I said, 'To hell with you as well!' These people don't make no conversation with you. They're not interested in talk. The only ones that'll talk are those that pick up a man. They'll talk with *him* all day long. If you're on your own in there, you're on your own. You couldn't make friends with no one. You might talk to a person and she'd just walk away.

Of course if they want something, that's different. Yesterday someone said, 'Oh Beatty! Got a cigarette?' Gave her a couple of cigarettes. Then a couple of minutes later she said, 'Oh Beatty! Lend me twenty pence.' I said, 'All right. Here you are, here's twenty pence.' Then another one come up. 'Got a cigarette, Beatty?' 'Oh,' I said, 'All right. Here you are, here's one.' Then as soon as I went in to the television someone said, 'Got a cigarette?' 'Oh Christ! All right. Here you are, have one!'

There's two smartly dressed sisters. They've been there thirty years. Just so—beads, hats and coats. Both go and have their hair done every week. Don't mix with anybody, keep theirselves to theirselves. They've got a room each. Their mother was there at first, a war widow—her husband was an officer in the Indian Army. The mother and one daughter had a room to theirselves, and the other daughter lived in the next room. Then the mother got too old and she became ill and she was too much to look after so they put her in hospital to build her body up and then they put her in an Old Ladies Home. She's over ninety. They're out all day long. After two or three hours visiting their mother they just come back at five o'clock ready for the half past five tea. Soon as they've had their tea they go up in their rooms. Won't have no conversation with anybody. Don't watch the telly, no nothing. Just say, 'Hello, how are you?' and that's all.

Some of the women are really sick. There's two or three that's had brain operations. Phyllis has had one. Mary's had one— she's always of a shake. They can't wash properly. There's one Major getting fed up with it. Oh she's very rough. You wouldn't think she was a Salvation Army Major. 'Come on! Get in the bath! Here you are, here's your flannel! Now get on with it! You look as if you've never had a wash all the week, you dirty beast!' Oh I couldn't be like that.

There's this girl Yvonne. She goes in the washroom six or seven times a day. All she can do is wash her hands. I should say she's about thirty-eight—she still sees what women see every month so she can't be very old. She's useless. A man couldn't put up with it. She couldn't fry an egg. She had this man for a bit, just for someone to talk to. Tall, slim man, smartly dressed, very nice and clean. I saw them in Hopetown Street once, in the car park. She was talking to him and smiling but she was edging away. Then, when she's edging more, he says, 'All right. Cheerio.' No, she wouldn't be no good to a man. It would be just hold hands and maybe kiss and cuddle. He'd have to wash her hair and bath her. She won't go into a coffee shop by herself. She'll call Joyce and if Joyce doesn't want to go she'll call Alice and if Alice doesn't want to go she'll call Minnie.

Minnie's all right if you're giving her money for cigarettes. This Yvonne when Minnie helps her says, 'Here you are, Minnie. Ten pence.' Well Minnie's then in her glory. 'Minnie!' 'Yes, what do you want?' 'Come on! In the bathroom! Put the plug in and run the water for me!' So Minnie runs the water till it's coming up to a certain height. 'All right. Get in.' So Yvonne gets in. She says, 'Minnie, will you wash my back?' So Minnie says, 'All right,' washes all her back. 'Now wash all my neck.' 'Now wash my face.' She does all that. 'Now my legs and my feet.' Minnie does all that—and that and that. Then Yvonne says, 'I'm going to get out now. Take away the plug.' So the dirty water's going away. Minnie washes the bath round, puts the plug in, runs the water to a certain height again. Yvonne gets in again and has a good rinse over. Finish. Out. Then

19

Minnie has to wipe all her back, everything, face and all. 'I'm all right, now, Minnie. I'm going to get my petticoat and my nightie and then I'm going to bed.'

Another time she happened to call Joyce who was in the yard. 'Joyce! I want you a minute!' So Joyce said, 'What do you want?' She said, 'Come in the washroom with me!' So Joyce went in the washroom with her. 'Joyce,' she said, 'would you wash my hair?' 'All right.' Joyce filled up the sink with hot water. 'Come, bend your head over.' She poured all water over her. Then she poured the shampoo and rubbed till all the dirt was off. She took away the plug and all the water run away. She filled up the sink with nice clean water over again. Another good rinse. Squeezed her hair till all the water was gone. Then she took the towel and rubbed all her hair and made it into a bun. 'Wait till it's a bit dry and when it's dry I'll comb it out.'

A woman once was in the washroom the same time as me. I said to her, 'Ooh, you look very rough today!' 'Yes,' she said, 'I feel rough.' So I said, 'Why don't you have a nice hot bath?' 'Oh no, no, no, no!' she said. I said, 'Why?' I said, 'I'll run the tap and get the bathwater ready for you, then I'll give you a bath.' 'No, no!' She just washed her hands and face. I said, 'Well, that ain't going to do you much good, love!' 'Oh it'll do,' she said. So I said, 'Don't you like a bath?' 'I haven't had a bath,' she said, 'for six weeks.' I said, 'What?!! Six weeks?!!' 'Yes,' she said. 'Oh,' I said, 'do have a bath!' 'Couldn't be bothered!'

I've been to the Welfare lady in Old Nichol Street. I don't want to be in the Salvation Army Hostel no more. It's making me ill. One morning when I see it was daylight I put on my dressing-gown and went through the yard and had a look at the clock outside the office. It was twenty to five. You're not supposed to get up till twenty to seven if you're not going to work, but I thought to myself, 'It's a lovely morning.' So I make my bed, go to the washroom, dress, lift the bolt up, out—and I was having a cup of tea in the coffee shop in Fournier Street at half past seven.

You see people die. There was a young woman that used to work in Mile End Road in a furniture shop. She'd been working there for years. She was a lovely woman with beautiful hair.

Come a time when this place closed down and she fretted over losing her job, she had no more interest in things and her body begin to deteriorate and deteriorate and she couldn't care less. She stood in the street and the rain would be pouring down on her. One evening I saw her sitting in the yard and it was teeming with rain. I said, 'Don't sit there, love! Why don't you go under the shelter?' And then the Brigadier come out and got hold of her, she said, 'Come on, go and sit in the dry!' The next day I saw her. I looked at her, I thought, 'Oh no! Something's going to happen! God forbid!' One part of her face was white, the other part was mauve. That same day she went to bed and she had a heart attack, she fell out of bed—thump. Someone went and fetched Tessa, one of the Salvation Army girls, and Tessa come up and sent for the Major. They put her back on the bed but she was already dead. She had starved herself to death. If you only saw her, your heart would have cried. To tell the truth *I* cried. When I saw that girl when she was working in Mile End her body was over twelve stone, and she went from twelve stone to six stone. Knowing she lost such a wonderful job when she was happy in that job she simply fretted inwardly and it preyed on her mind.

Then there was this old lady brought in. She come out of hospital and she went back to her place but her place was locked up and she walked around for three weeks and she was found wandering around and she was brought in by the police on a Sunday night. If you saw that woman—well, I cried. I hugged her, I said, 'Oh Mum! I wish I could do something for you! What's your name, love?' She said, 'My name's Cathy.' She had asthma. You imagine someone sixty walking around for three weeks with asthma—no sleep, no food, no nothing! I was taking her to the canteen to see if she could have tea, and the Major come behind us. 'Come along! Get a move on!' I said, 'Oh my God! You've got no sympathy?! She's only got one eye! Don't talk to her like that! It might happen to *you* one day. But I don't wish you any harm. God forbid.' I took her and I helped the tea to her lips. She said, 'I can't, Beatty,' so I took her to her bed. She went to bed. And on the Monday I'm looking and looking. Come five o'clock I went to her and I said, 'Do you want a cup of tea, Mum?' She said, 'No.' Then the Major come, had a look, took her in the office and sat with her for half an hour while she was fighting for her breath. Then when the poor lady's life was gone they called the doctor and the body was took away to the mortuary.

Then one Friday about quarter to six something seemed to say, 'Beatty, go in the bedroom!' This woman—Lily her name was—big stout woman who slept in the bed opposite mine—she worked in the kitchen in the Mint for eight years—she come home that night on the Friday, went in the canteen had something to eat, came out and went in the bedroom. I went in and found her lying on the floor. 'Lily! What's wrong!' She was fighting for her breath. I thought to myself, 'Perhaps she's in a fit.' I went and got the Captain. I said, 'Quick, Captain! Lily's in a fit I think. She's fighting for her breath.' She said, 'I've got to serve supper.' 'Oh,' I said, 'do please come! Just for a minute. Please!' So she did, and we lifted Lily on the bed. Then she went away again to serve the suppers. 'I'll come back later,' she said. I waited and waited, then I run to the office and fetched the Brigadier. I said, 'You'd better come quick,' and she and the Captain come running. They said, 'What shall we do—send for the doctor or the ambulance?' I said, 'You'd better send for the ambulance. This is Emergency.'

So the Brigadier rung for the ambulance. 'Please send an ambulance to the Salvation Army Hostel, Hopetown Street.' Two men came. They looked at Lily. I said to one of them, 'Excuse me,' I said, 'she's got false teeth.' So he took the false teeth out and he looked at his friend and he said, 'Come on,' he said, 'we'd better hurry up!' The other one said, 'She's finished but we must take her.'

She was already dead by the time they got her on a stretcher to the gate.

TWO

Michael and Derek, my two boys, are ashamed to think that their Mum went into a Salvation Army Hostel.

I met Derek eight years ago in Cheshire Street Market after a gap of two or three years. I said, 'Derek, come. Let's have a cup of tea.' He said, 'I've got no money, Mum.' I said, 'I pay.' So the two together we sat down and had a cup of tea and after this cup of tea we come out. I said, 'All right then, Derek. I'll see you again, love. I'm going this way. You go that way.' And I've never seen my son Derek after that.

He married a girl called Sheila from Hackney Road. He happened to go into this coffee shop in Hackney Road and she was sitting at a table and they got chatting together. She made cardboard boxes for shirts. Her mother and father had ten children—five sons and five daughters. Sheila was the youngest of the five daughters. She and my son Derek got married in Shoreditch Town Hall.

When they was married for twelve to thirteen years and for the first time Sheila was nine months pregnant, her father got very ill and was rushed to the London Hospital. It was getting near Christmas and he asked to see the whole of the family. 'I want to see my daughters, my grandchildren, everybody.' Everybody come round the bed. Sheila put her arm round him and she said, 'We want to see you well, love.' 'Yes,' he said, 'I know, Sheila, and I've got something for you but you mustn't open it until your baby is born.' It was a box of baby clothes wrapped in ribbon. 'I wish you and Derek all the luck in the world. Cheerio.' Then he looked at everyone and smiled at them. 'All right, Dad.' 'Cheerio, Dad.' 'God bless you.' 'Hope see you Christmas.' But Christmas coming—finish.

Sheila was upset and she was going to have this baby. Derek got back one day from the upholstery factory where he was working. He opened the door. Sheila was in labour. He cried, 'Oh my God! My wife! What can I do?!' He lifted her up. He carried her down one flight of stairs, then another, then another. A friend opposite who had a mini-cab he said, 'Derek, what's wrong?' He helped Derek get Sheila into the mini-cab and they rushed her to the Bethnal Green Hospital. She was took in the maternity ward.

My son is walking up and down, up and down, up and down, down, up. Then he sees two doctors coming out and two sisters coming out and a nurse. One of the doctors comes to my son. Derek asks, 'Doctor, is my wife all right?' The doctor says, 'Yes, but I'm very very sorry, Mr Ali, your wife has lost the baby that you hoped you'd save.' After then my son passed out, he didn't know no more for maybe it was one hour, maybe two. When he went into the ward he said, 'Never mind, Sheila. Maybe we will have luck next time. Maybe what has happened was to be. Only Up Above knows and nobody else.'

When Sheila got better and she was coming out of hospital the Guvnor at work said to Derek, 'The factory's coming down, but don't worry, Derek, you and your wife and me and my wife will go to the New Town in Suffolk. I'm giving you a house with the same job there.' So my son went to Suffolk with Sheila.

Michael met his wife Ann when he was working in a brooch factory in Leman Street. She was coming down the stairs and she looked at my son and he looked at her and she said, 'Are you going anywhere tonight? I'd like to meet you.' 'Well,' he said, 'if you like I'll meet you at seven o'clock. Here's my address.' She knocked on the door, she come in and I gave her a piece of cake and a cup of tea. And that went on for about a year and then they decided to get engaged.

Then Ann's father wanted to interview Michael in his sitting-room because he was very strict. He come from Liverpool—Mr Murphy. Mr and Mrs Murphy was very nice but I couldn't understand them. They spoke everything in Gaelic. It's a very hard language. If you stayed with the mother and father for two or three years even, you couldn't pick it up. You see Irish-

24

men sitting talking Gaelic sometimes in Georgina's. You can guess what a Bangladesh person is talking, but not a person talking Gaelic.

So Michael went out and bought himself a suit and new shirt, new shoes, everything, and he went down to see the mother and the father in Lukin Street, and the father said to him, 'Look, Michael, you're going out with my daughter. If you wan't to get engaged to her you'll have to prove you'll be a good husband and father, prove that you're going to be a man.' Michael said, 'I'm not a lay around, Mr Murphy! You know that! I'm a man for my job, and if you'll let me get engaged to your daughter I'll prove that I'm going to be a man.'

And he's done it, he's done it—he's stuck to his word! When he married Mr Murphy's daughter, Mr Murphy was working down at the Wapping Docks and he give him a job with him unloading the boats and loading them up again right until they had their redundancy. Soon after that Michael got a job in the Betts Street Baths and when they was condemned they sent him to the Cable Street Highway Baths. He's a swimming instructor there and he works for an Indian bank as well.

He gets up four o'clock and he goes over to the bank half past. He bumps all the floors with polish and he does all the landings, the men's toilets, the passages and the corridors and the stairs, and he puts the dust out in the street for the dust people. When the women come on at five o'clock, all they've got to do is go round with the polishing machines—finish, finish, finish. While they're doing that, my son puts the kettle on and he makes everybody a cup of tea and calls them. 'Come along, ladies, here's your cup of tea.' 'Here's your cup of tea, Mum.' 'A cup of tea for you, Gran.' 'A cup of tea for you, love.' 'Here's your biscuits.' 'I'm going home now to see my four children and my wife.' 'Cheerio, Michael!'

He had to get four references for that job. The Guvnor got on the phone to them—'Yes, this boy's worked for me for so long.' . . . 'Yes, he's a very nice boy, very trustworthy.' He said, 'Here you are then, Michael. Here's the keys to get into the office and to open the street door. Bolt it as soon as you get in and do what you've got to do upstairs. I'll give you twenty pound a week clear. How would you like that, Michael?' 'Yes, sir.

Thank you very much.' That twenty pound he don't touch. He puts it away in the bank.

He gets home from the bank half past eight, puts the kettle on, makes his wife a cup of tea, makes his four children a cup of tea. 'Here you are Ann, a cup of tea for you, love. Ruth, Wayne, Anabella, Jane . . . Tea, love?' 'Yes, Daddy. Oh you are a very good Daddy.' 'Yes, because I love you very much. You are my lovers. You are everything to me.'

Ann goes and does a little job in a packing factory from nine o'clock till four o'clock. She gets eight pound a week for that and that eight pound goes in the Post Office for the children when they grow older. Then she runs a Clothing Club. She gets commission for that. Then two of the children go and do a job Saturday morning on a stall in the market.

Michael used to weigh sixteen stone. He used to be a weight-lifter, a muscleman lifting the bar. But by teaching swimming he's gone right down to twelve stone. Out of his wages every week at the Baths he puts four pound aside in boxes—a pound for his son and a pound each for his girls.

Six months ago he saved a little boy's life. He was standing rolling himself a cigarette. 'Oh my God!' Shoes off. He had to swim right out. The boy was in trouble in the deep end. He brought him right to the bank on his shoulders and laid him out flat and had to give him the kiss of life. After the little boy woke up he said, 'Thank you.' He could hardly talk. Then someone came with a hot drink which seemed to warm his chest up. He said, 'I feel ever so much better.' But he was a bit shaken. My son wrapped a blanket around him and asked him, 'Where do you live, son?' 'Oh,' he said, 'I live a long way—the Old Kent Road, in the Buildings.' So my son said, 'Well, never mind. You sit there for quarter of an hour, twenty minutes. I'll call a mini-cab.'

He called the mini-cab and he laid this boy down flat on the back seat and he sat there with the boy's head on his lap. The mini-cab was going and going and going and going, and round a corner and round a corner was a big block of flats and the boy said to my son, 'I live there!' My son stopped the cab and asked the driver how much. He said, 'One pound.' So he gave him a pound for the journey and twenty pence tip. And then he lifted the boy and carried him seven floors up, knocked on the door and the mother come, she said, 'Oh my God!' He said, 'Nothing to worry about, love, but your boy tried to get to the deep end and he couldn't make it. He got in a bit of difficulty and I had to bring him from the water to the side and give him the kiss of life.' The boy said, 'I'm all right, Mum!' My son took him in and laid him on a couch and then the mother said to my son, 'Would you like a cup of tea?' so my son said, 'Well, I wouldn't mind. But if it's too much trouble, don't bother.' 'No, no, no!' So she made him a cup of tea and then she said, 'Do you smoke?' He said, 'No, madam, no. You need it more than me. Look at the children you've got. Aren't they lovely?' 'Don't worry yourself,' she said. 'You're very very good to bring my son home. Here you are. Take this cigarette. Enjoy it.'

Three weeks later the boy come to the swimming baths with his father and my son heard someone calling, 'Michael! Michael!' The boy introduced him to his father and the father said, 'Thank you ever so much for saving my son's life.' 'Well,' Michael said, 'I had to. I've got four children of my own.' Then the boy said, 'I've brought you a present, Michael. Ten cigarettes.' He said, 'You shouldn't have done that, son. Anyhow I'm pleased!' and he asked the boy his address in full and six weeks later he sent the mother a three pound cheque. 'Dear Friend, I'm sending three pound for the boy that I saved to make a little party with his brothers and sisters.' He's been promoted since then and he's asked a friend to learn him how to drive a car and he's passed his test so he's bought himself a car.

Michael said to me once, 'What we don't have now when we're young I'm going to make up for when I'm married.' And he did. He lives at 14 —— House, —— Street, near Arbour Square, and if you saw his home you'd have a big shock because it's a wonderful home he's got. All his own money. All his own hands. Nobody helped him. He's done it to please his wife. He loves his wife very, very much. It was love for him the first time he saw this girl and she was the only girl he ever had. She's very house proud. She likes things that are nice. What goes, goes, and he's got to do it. She likes to feel that she's living clean and not living in shit. A pair of shoes for one of the children—eight guineas. Well I don't blame her. You only live once.

He's painted all the ceilings apple green and over one way is one colour paint and over the other way is different paint. And in the great big sitting-room he's made a partition, a high wall with all bamboo sticks and brown paper, four pounds a roll, and in the corner he's got a kind of snake made of bamboo with every kind of potted plant on it—one and one and one and one. Then there's a coloured television and a round wine cabinet, a map of the world, (eighty-six guineas he paid for that). The three piece suite was a hundred and sixty guineas. In the lounge he's got a white table and four white chairs to go with the table. Upstairs there's a battery television for the children. If they've got schoolmates in he says, 'Go on now! Upstairs!' Then he's bought two dogs with all hair in front that cost him thirty-five guineas each. He wants to breed pups. I've been out in the garden. He's dug it all up and he's made like a border all round, and in the middle deep down he's made a fish pond and a pipe with clean water running through. He's a very handy boy, he is.

I go to see him every week, but he's a boy now that only likes his wife and children round him. One night I was watching the television there and there was a film and I was getting so interested in this film that the time was getting on and I think I'd been there for about three hours. So he looked over and he said, 'Mum,' he said, 'I don't think you want to go home tonight, do you?' He said, 'When you come here you make a meal of it,' he said. I said, 'All right then, Michael. I'm going home now.' He said, 'I don't mind you coming down,' he said, 'if it's only for half an hour,' he said, 'but when you come you want to sit here all night and I don't like it.' In other words, really and truly, my son Michael and my daughter-in-law Ann, they don't want me there at all. I went round one day and I told Michael I needed a few shillings. He said, 'No. You're a fucking nuisance!' There's not many boys would say that to their mother. Another time I asked him he said, 'Sorry, Mum. I haven't got one penny, love. Three of the children have gone to Spain for two weeks holiday. All money gone, love. What can I do? Now, if you don't mind, we're going out.' ' Oh don't worry son,' I said. 'I'll see what I can do. Go out and enjoy yourself.' Couldn't get a halfpenny. Walked home. They don't want much to do with me. They never come to see me though they've got the car.

They've even changed their name by deed poll. But that's because at school they used to call Ruth, the eldest one, 'Ali Baba'. They said, 'Your father's coloured!' It disheartened her and she went home and she cried and cried and cried. She was only eight. Michael had never seen her cry like that before. He said, 'What's wrong, Ruth? Tell Daddy what's wrong!' She said, 'I don't want the name "Ali" no more!' He said, 'Don't worry, Ruth. I'll change the name to a new name, love, and then you'll be all right.' Derek's changed his name now too.

Michael's more the colour of his father. Derek's white like me. I met Basit after I come from Luton to London. He was eighteen, only a young boy. I was twenty and I was working as a chamber maid in a bed and breakfast hotel. I read about this job in a Luton paper. 'CHAMBER MAID WANTED. TAVISTOCK SQUARE, LONDON.' I said to my mother, 'I'm going to write after that job,' and I got it. I'd to go round with a shoe-box polishing the shoes left outside the doors. Then I'd see to everybody's breakfast on a tray, wait till they'd finished, go down, wash all up. Then when they was gone out I'd go upstairs and do all the rooms—hoover, do all the dusting and make the beds. Six o'clock till four.

There was another young woman working in the hotel and this other young woman had friends, a husband and wife, in No. 11, Casson Street in the East End. She said to me, 'Beatty,' she said, 'would you mind coming with me to these friends of mine?' I said, 'I don't mind.' So we went.

This fellow that I married lived in the next room. He happened to knock on the door, come in, and he was offered a cup of tea. Basit his name was. He was a seaman from East Pakistan. He was five-foot-four, a little short fellow with a nice body. He'd brown eyes, olive skin, nice face, nice black wavy hair. He was a Muslim and he spoke good English, and he carried a paper to show he was a British subject. I'd never seen a coloured man before in my life!

Well, while he was drinking his tea, he kept looking at me so my friend said, 'What does he keep looking at you for, Beatty?' I said, 'I don't know,' I said. 'I don't want him just the same.' So she said, 'He's not a bad looking fellow, you know, Beatty.' I said, 'I know that but I don't want him.' When we come out he followed us into the street right to the bus stop, and he wanted to get on the bus with us but the bus went off quick so he couldn't get on. My friend said, 'Don't you like coloured people, Beatty?' I said, 'I don't think they'd be any good.' She said, 'Well you don't know. You can't class everybody the same, Beatty,' she said. She said, 'Everybody's got ten fingers but no finger's the same.'

Well we went back another time and he came in the room again. And that was going on for nearly a year till the time come he said, 'Would you like to come and live with me and get married?' 'Ooh,' I said, 'I don't know.' 'I'll be good to you,' he said. Anyway, my friend left this job in Tavistock Square and got married, and I stayed on another few weeks and then I left and got married to Basit—in 1936 in Limehouse Registry Office, Poplar. No honeymoon, nothing like that. No party. Just a quiet wedding. Go in and get married, and out and home, finish. I made a big mistake. When I fell for Derek in 1937, I was ten days in hospital and Basit only come to see me once and all he brought me was an apple. Then when I fell for Michael in 1942 I'd to go next door and call for the ambulance myself.

I said to Basit before we was married. 'I don't think you'd be any good to me.' He said, 'You haven't tried me. You don't know, do you?' Well I know now. Some husbands show appreciation to their wives. 'Oh hello, darling! You've been busy today? You look tired. Sit down and I'll make you a cup of tea.' But with Basit it was me doing everything—cooking, cleaning, washing, ironing. That man never worried for anything. 'Here you are. Have your food.' Took away the plate. More food. Take away the plate, wash it up. 'Cup of tea!' 'Here you are. A cup of tea.' There was no affection. When he left the sea he never come home on a Friday night like other husbands and said, 'Here you are, love. A nice box of sweets (or a nice packet of cigarettes).' Nothing like that. Every morning for thirty years a cup of tea and toast in the bed. And he never washed a cup! How you left the flat in the morning you went home and found it just the same, and sometimes he was still laying in the bed. If he wanted to go out and do a day's work he would go out and do a day's work, otherwise he wouldn't. He used to say, 'Look,

Beatty, you're working, you're getting wages, so what money you're earning you can buy food with that, you can pay the rent with that. What more do you want?' I tried him once for two or three weeks to see if he'd go to work if I didn't. But he wouldn't. When I look around and see what some husbands do for their wives! People used to say to me, 'Well, Beatty, I think you're ever so good to your husband because you never worry him for nothing. He never buys you anything. He don't buy you a packet of fags and he's never bought no clothes for you, and from the time that you carried for them two children you was working all the time.' I didn't worry that man for a penny piece. I didn't worry him for nothing for the two children from the time they were born till the time they went to school and they left school and they picked up a girl and got married. Truly it don't make sense. None.

I went out once and I come back with a great big bunch of tulips. I put so many here, so many here and so many there. All of a sudden the key come in the door and as soon as Basit saw the flowers he said, 'Come on,' he said, 'all them lot's got to be chucked away!' He wouldn't have a flower indoors. I said, 'Why?' He said, 'We don't like flowers indoors. That's very bad luck.' So he lifted up the window and he chucked every one of them out into the street. Crikey! All the lot went. None of the Bangladesh people will have flowers. And yet they like artificial flowers. If you go into a Bangladesh house you always see a bunch of artificial flowers. You never see real flowers. They've got them strung over this way and over that way and across the roof.

I've got a plant at the hostel. A man give it to me. I was going down the side turning beside Booth House. They've got a great big back yard, and there was all these plants all in a line on a wall. Some of them was in flower. Oh they was beautiful! I said to this man who was tending them, 'That's some nice plants you've got.' Then I saw this one. It was all dead. I said, 'That little one looks very poorly, don't it? I wouldn't mind taking it.' He said, 'All right. I don't want it. If you can do anything with it, take it, love, by all means. You're welcome to it.' So I took it. Then I went and got half a carrier bag of mould from Back Church Lane Park, dug it up with my hands. Then I went back to the Salvation Army, held this plant up, took all the hard soil off and chucked it into the bin. Then I put some soil in the bottom of the pot, then put the plant in and worked my way round till the soil come to the top, and I patted it round. It's one of them plants that when they get big they hang down. But it'll take years for that. Little green leaves. I keep it on the window-ledge in the yard. They've got more, about fifty pots on black long boxes—a pot here and a pot there. Oh lots. Some have little red flowers, red, red, and red. Oh yes, they like flowers in the Salvation Army Hostel. There's one woman there, she buys a big bunch every week for the meeting they have every Sunday from three to four in the canteen. Costs her about fifty pence. The meeting's all about God. I never go. I feel more at ease in Christ Church Hall, Hanbury Street. In the Salvation Army Hostel you're not at rest. Your body feels different. But when you go into Christ Church and sit and hear the lady play the piano then you've got more confidence.

They've got two white sort of vases in the hostel, flat at the bottom, then coming up with a stem, then big and round with like green trees in them. The Brigadier's got rid of the plants that was in them before. Big mauve blooms they had. The cat jumped onto them and broke them. He ate the leaves. Black and white he is. I've seen him catch two rats. They weren't half wallopers and all. They come from the bombed ruin where the cars are at the side. They was monsters. He flew after them, caught them by the neck, played around with them and killed them. But he didn't eat them. He left them. I like cats. Some-times I go out and buy him a tin of Kit-e-Kat, sometimes a pint of milk.

I like all animals. I go out every morning and I buy a loaf and I feed all the birds—the pigeons and the sparrows. I used to have two budgerigars and they could talk. 'Whistle!' 'Look!' 'Good morning!' My Michael used to go mad for pigeons. He had two racing pigeons. He made a great big cage for them. He ended up with twenty. Then he come home one day with a cardboard box. I said, 'What's this?' Blimey, when I opened it, it's only two tame mice! 'Good God!' I said. 'Take them away!' He said, 'They're all right, Mum. Let them run around.' Oh what a laugh! I couldn't stop laughing. One run round this way.

The other one run round that way. And when they was tired they come the two together. One met with an accident. It got caught in the door.

Victoria Park is gorgeous. They've animals there. When my husband left me I used to go over with a great big carrier of stuff every Sunday regular. Fed all the rabbits with cabbage and carrots, and the deers with bread and cake and biscuits. They used to come running and nibble it all. Then there was a great big grey animal with three legs that used to hop as soon as you put the food down, but until then he was very shy and used to sit in a corner.

I like Trafalgar Square as well. I like a ride over there sometimes. Take a lot of bread in a carrier bag and break it up for the pigeons. Then it's a nice ride to Hyde Park, Regent's Park, Battersea Park. . . . If I ain't got no money I show the conductor the pension book. They say, 'What? Are you waiting for your permit?' I say, 'Yes.'

Jumped on a bus the other day. Oh it was lovely! Beautiful! Never cost me a penny. Come to the end of the ride and then went right back where we come from. The conductor said, 'You're having a long ride, madam.' I said, 'Yes, I've got nothing to do.' He said, 'You're enjoying yourself. I can see you are!' I said, 'Why not?! Make the best of it, get cracking!'

Same as another day. Jumped on a 25 bus and went all the way to Hyde Park. 'Fare, madam.' 'Here you are—the Pension Book.' This bloke he wouldn't really believe me, he said, 'I think you're having me on!' He said, 'How old are you?' I said, 'Sixty.' He said, 'No! Never! You're not that age, love!' I said, 'I *am*! Next time I'll bring my birth certificate!' 'Well,' he said, 'if that's your age, love, then you must have kept yourself very good when you was young!'

He was right, though everybody used to go mad for me. When I was a young girl and I was working in Old Bedford Road Hospital, Luton, there was this kitchen porter, dark brown hair, short, very thin. Every time he spotted me he used to stand looking. One day he said to me, 'When's your day off, Beatty?' I said, 'Tomorrow.' He said, 'Funny thing. It's my day off as well. I'll be waiting for you outside.' I said, 'You won't, you know!' He said, 'I bet I *will*!' and when I went out there he stood waiting. I said, 'All right,' so we went for a walk round and then I took him home. My mum liked him. 'Nice boy, Beatty.' I was eleven. He was twenty-two.

THREE

My father Alfred Webster come from Scotland—him and his brother Albert. Oh he had a wicked temper! We had to be in at a certain time and if we wasn't in at a certain time then we used to get a good whack round the shoulders. 'If I told you to be in here at ten o'clock, I want you in here at ten o'clock!'

He kept two butcher's shops on the go—one in Wellington Street and one near Chapel Street Market. Every Monday him and his brother used to go to the market and bring back bullocks and sheep and pigs to be slaughtered in the big slaughter house in Windsor Walk near where we lived. And on Tuesdays they used to walk from Luton to Hitchin and do the same thing, him with a sheep dog and a stick on one side of the road, and his brother with a sheep dog and a stick on the other side of the road. Every week-end he used to give all the old people in our street a free joint of meat. On Saturday we used to load up the van. 'Your meat, love.' 'Here's your meat, Mum, for the week-end.'

He liked reading the paper. That was his hobby—the paper and horse-racing. Sometimes of a Saturday night he'd say to my mother, 'I think I'll go out and have a drink, May,' and she'd say, 'All right, Alf. Go on. You go out and have a drink with your brother.' And afterwards his brother used to come back with him and have his supper and then go home.

My mother worked in the Alma Cinema in Manchester Street, cleaning. In the morningtime she used to do cleaning, and afternoon she used to do cleaning. She also helped the poor. If she thought the poor wanted cleaning done, washing done, she'd do it. She used to send me to knock on their doors. 'You want your washing done today, Mum?' 'Yes, take it,' and I'd take their things home to 51, Windsor Street and we'd give them a good wash on the board, boil them, rinse them, hang them in the yard, dry them, press them, fold them, put their name. 'Here you are, Mum. Here's your washing.' Next door do the same. Then me and my two sisters and my brother used to go round and ask people in the street if they wanted any errands fetched or did they want any housework done or window cleaning done or their garden dug up or plants planted for a shilling. And my brother Derek—oh God bless him—if anybody needed their shoes done, he'd mend them, and he used to go for boxes of wood for people, chop them up, make sticks, knock on their doors. 'Here you are, Mum. Here's your wood.'

I was in the same school from the age of five right till I was fourteen. We done lessons in the morning and then in the afternoon we learned how to do washing clothes, how to do gardening, how to do cooking, how to make pastry.

One day, when the time was going on and on, and Derek was eleven and I was eight and Minnie was nine and Dorothy was ten, we all went to Old Bedford Road Hospital and Workhouse. When we walked in the matron come towards us, she said, 'You're four bonny and strong children!' I said, 'Yes, because my father comes from Scotland and he's very strict.' So she asked me, 'What have you come for? Have you come to see a patient?' I said, 'No. Our father doesn't want us to roam around in the streets and we feel we'd like to come and help you and those that need us. Are there any odd jobs?' She said, 'Yes,' and we worked there right until we left school from four till ten in term-time and all day Saturday and in the holidays. Sunday we helped the poor.

You see, we was brought up the hard way. That is why people cannot understand me now. Because my husband left me and didn't want me any more, people was running away with the idea 'Mrs Ali, how are you going to live now?'. I said, 'I'm well trained. I've been brought up the hard way, not the soft way.'

Derek helped make the medicines and Minnie helped in the laundry and Dorothy made herself useful going round doing all the dusting and serving out meals, and I looked after patients. I'd get them out into their wheelchairs and while they were sitting out for about a quarter of an hour I'd shift the bed and make it all nice and clean and then me and the nurse in the ward we'd lift the old lady in the bed and I'd ask the old lady if she wanted anything like tea, coffee or milk. I wore an overall for dirty work and when it came to food I took that off and put a clean one on. Two blue overalls a day.

I'll never forget it,—I was only ten or a little bit older at the time—there was a woman that was paralysed from the neck down, a great big woman. She was in a cot in case she was to roll out and roll on the floor. I was helping to give out the food and wash the old ladies, make their beds in this ward, and I happened to see this old lady. I said, 'Hello, Mum. You all right?' 'Yes, Beatty.' 'Do you want anything, love?' 'Well I'd like a drop of water, if you don't mind.' And I went and got her a lovely glass of water. I lifted the side of the bed down and I knelt down on the floor and held her head. 'Take your time. Aah! All right, Mum?' 'Yes.' 'Another little drop?' 'Yes.' 'Take your time, love. All right? All right? Another little drop? All right? Another little drop?' The glass was nearly finished. 'Do you want any more?' 'No, love. Thank you ever so much. God bless you.'

They wouldn't do that for you at the Salvation Army Hostel. Oh no.

We all had a pound a week. My sister had a pound, I had a pound, my other sister had a pound and my brother had a pound. We'd come home on a Friday after nine and say, 'Here you are, Mum. Here's three pound for you and five shillings for each of us.'

At the end of one year my brother knew how to make medicines. He passed a test. Then he wanted to learn the injections. He passed the test. The head doctor called him one day in his office, he said, 'Well, son, what is your nationality?' 'My father come from Scotland, sir.' 'And your mother?' 'From Manor Park, Ilford.' 'And how old are you?' 'I'm only thirteen, doctor.' He said, '*How* old?! *Thirteen*?!!' He said, 'Well I think you are a very, very clever boy.' He said, 'To think that you started in this hospital at eleven, love, and you learned to make medicine in one year, well I think you're wonderful. Then you've learned to do the injections. I think you deserve a gold medal for that, love.' He said, 'What kind of a school do you go to?' 'Only an ordinary school, sir.' 'Well,' he said, 'you must have a good brain. Do you take after your mother or your father?' 'After my father, sir. If I do anything wrong indoors he gives me the belt.'

In the end Derek learned how to do an operation on a wax model, how to do the carving and the stitching. That took him a very long time but he was a qualified doctor at the age of twenty-five and he didn't have to go to Medical School because he had brains.

They had a big clean up at the hospital once. The matron said, 'Beatty, we're going to be busy today, love. You don't mind a little bit of hard work, do you?' I said, 'No, not at all.' We took the mattresses right off from the beds and where the springs went into the joists—here and there and here and here—we took them up and we rubbed and rubbed everything with paraffin and then done it all down with a cloth till it was nice and clean. Then we shook the mattresses and put them back on, and then we polished all the frames.

The Matron's quarters was ever so nice. Lovely big bathroom and toilet. Lovely big staircase with carpet down it. Enormous sitting room. Her two daughters had a great big double room to theirselves upstairs. Her son had a big room to hisself. And her mother had a big room to herself. And she and her husband had a big double room to theirselves. All the rooms was fitted with carpet. You opened the door of the dining-room and went down a long passage and there was the kitchen with a big gas oven for keeping the food hot which come from the hospital kitchen.

One time her maid went on holiday and I took over her job. I used to clean all their shoes every morning, scrape the mud off with a knife and then polish them. They used to buzz the bell for food. I'd take it in on a tray, put it on the side, take everything off and put it in the middle of the table and then walk out. I wore a uniform. The matron said, 'I'm going to rig you out, Beatty.' Brown dress. Little chocolate apron. Little cap—brown band and white lace. She said, 'Now look at yourself in the glass. You look lovely.' I'd long wavy hair. Her husband liked me and all. A very tall gentleman. 'Morning,

Beatty. You all right?' 'Yes, sir. You all right?' 'Yes.'

The maid was on holiday for two weeks. When she come back she said to the matron, 'My God this place has been kept lovely!' 'Oh yes,' says the matron, 'we've had a young girl in here.' Then the maid said, 'Who *is* this young girl?! I'd like to see her.' So the matron come over where I was working in the hospital and she called me in the office. She said, 'Beatty,' she said, 'you know that maid that was gone on the two weeks' holiday? She wants to see you.' I said, 'She wants to see *me*?! What for?!' She said, 'Because you've kept the place so nice and clean she thinks that you should come over and give her help.' I said, 'All right. I'll help her. I don't mind.' So I used to go over and help her every morning. She used to give me a few bob on the quiet. She said, 'You're a good little worker.'

Well we all left school. Derek stayed on at the hospital because he wanted to be a doctor. Minnie went to Birmingham. Dorothy—she was a very pretty girl, my sister Dorothy. She had a lovely body. She had a lovely face—she picked up a doctor that had money and she married him and she went to live at No 8, Garrick Road, Hendon. I worked on a machine in Hubbard's hat factory down Boot Street till I got fed up with that and went back to the hospital helping the matron and the nurses like before, but with bed and board. I'd a lovely bedroom —fitted carpet, chair, wardrobe, dressing table. I was paid about three pound a week. Them days was different. Three pound was a lot of money. You could go in a shop and get ten cigarettes and a box of matches for fourpence, and a cup of jam for a penny. Half a pound of sugar was only three ha'pence.

I stayed at the hospital till I was nineteen and I saw this sleeping-in job advertised in Tavistock Square, London.

One day after I went to London my father said to my Mum, 'Mum, I want to go and have a lay down for half an hour. Call me at five o'clock.' She went and called him. 'Alf! Alf!' He never woke up. That was the end. And his brother died soon after because they was always together. My sister Dorothy in Hendon, when she knew that Dad was gone, she was talking with her husband, she said, 'Look, my Mum looked for me when I was a baby and I'm going to look for her now.' He said, 'All right, Dorothy. If you feel that way, love, we'll go and see your Mum.'

And that's what they done. They went to see Mum all on her own. A knock come on the door. Mum opened the door and she see her daughter and her son-in-law and she hugged them and the husband says, 'Look, Mum, you're coming to live with us, love. You looked for your daughter when she was a baby. Now it's come to the time to look for you.' And my Mum went to the door again and she happened to see a husband and wife coming along with three children and two big suitcases and they was looking all round and she stopped them, she said, 'I think you're looking for a place.' The woman said, 'Yes.' 'Well,' said my Mum, 'Don't walk any more because you can have this house.' The man said, 'You must be joking!' My Mum said, 'No, I mean it. You come in and have a look round and see if you like it.' So she showed them upstairs, the two big bedrooms, then, coming downstairs, the big front room and big kitchen and outside the big garden with a toilet at the end, eight shillings a week rent. 'Well,' said the man, 'You're very good, Mrs Webster. Nobody else would give me a home like this. I must give you some money in return.' She said, 'No, you need it more than me, you've got three young children. What money you would want to give me, you spend on them.' And so she went to No 8, Garrick Road, Hendon, to my married sister, Dorothy.

Dorothy fell for a baby and when the baby was born she said to my Mum, 'Well, Mum,' she said, 'I want to go and do a little part-time job. Do you think you can manage the flat?' So Mum said, 'All right,' she said, 'I don't mind,' and she managed the flat and she looked for this baby from the time it was two weeks old till the time it was seven. She used to see the little boy to school and fetch him home, but come a time when she never turned up and the little boy run home from school and he couldn't make out why his Nanny never opened the door so he looked through the letter-box. 'Oh my God! My Nanny's on the floor!' He run next door and asked the gentleman, he said, 'I'm very sorry to worry you, mister, but my Nanny's on the floor and I can't get in.' So the gentleman had to force the back door and he lifted my Mum and carried her upstairs and the little son phoned for the doctor and the doctor come and he said, 'I'm very sorry, son,' he said, 'but your Nannie will never walk again. She's paralysed.' And while he was examining my Mum the little

40

boy went in the kitchen, put two cups of tea on the tray, sugar, milk and a plate of biscuits, and he took it in to the room. The doctor said, 'How old are you?' He said, 'I'm seven.' 'Well,' said the doctor, 'I think you're a very clever boy and I wish you all the luck in the world.'

Mum was paralysed for the next ten years and I was going over every week to help to feed her. She died in 1947. That was when she looked at me and my two sisters and my brother and she said, 'Beatty and Minnie and Dorothy and Derek, I'm going into the New World. If anybody needs any help from anywhere please help them. Never say no. What you do for people will be paid back in another way.'

When my husband run away and left me in 1965 someone recommended me to take a ride up the West End. She said, 'Beatty, why don't you go to Oxford Street? There's a fortune-teller there that's come from Brighton and she's very good.' I said, 'How much does she charge?' She said, 'Fifteen shillings.' I said, 'Well I wouldn't mind paying fifteen shillings.'

So I went upstairs, sat in a lovely sitting-room, all covered chairs. Then this elderly lady come out, she said, 'You're next.' So I stood up, made my way into the other room. 'Well,' she said, 'before we start I can tell you straight away that you're not going to win a fortune, love.' Then she shut the door, she looked at me and she looked through the crystal and she turned round and told me everything what had happened before I could tell her anything. She said, 'You're married to a coloured man, ain't you?' I said, 'Yes, that's right.' 'But he's never been any good to you, has he?' I said, 'No, that's right.' She said, 'He run away with a lot of money, didn't he?' I said, 'Yes, that's right.' She said, 'You've got two sons married, haven't you?' I said, 'Yes, that's right.' She said, 'One son's got children but the other son's got no children.' And I hadn't turned round and told her nothing!

After the crystal she looked at my hand, she said, 'You've been a very unlucky woman in your time,' she said. 'I think in the future you may be luckier but not yet awhile. It'll be a very long time.' Then she shuffled up the cards. She said, 'The cards look very good but for the moment you're going to have a very tough time. Your life's been hard right from the time that you was born right until now. It's never been easy, has it?' I said, 'No.' She said, 'You've got two sisters and a brother, haven't you?' I said, 'Yes, that's right.' She said, 'They're married now, ain't they? I don't know what's happened to your brother but I think he's in a living-in job somewhere. You've never seen your sisters and your brother for a long, long time, have you?' I said, 'That's right.' She said, 'You've lost your mother and father, haven't you?' I said, 'Yes, that's right.' 'And you lost your mother in 1947.' I said, 'Yes, that's right?' *How did she know that?!!*

FOUR

People was more genuine and more happy in Luton. You wouldn't sit by yourself indoors for hours and hours. A knock would come at the door. 'Come round. Make yourself a cup of tea. Cut yourself a piece of cake. Make yourself a sandwich. Do you want a dinner? Sit down. We'll give you a dinner.'

In Luton, many and many a time, my Mum used to be indoors on her own when Dad was out, and Mrs Turner next door would say, 'Come on, Mrs Webster! Don't sit in there! Come along, love! Have a cup of tea! Make yourself at home! Do you want anything to eat?' You never got that in London except in the war. When the war wasn't on everybody was for theirselves and, as the years go by, at all the places where I've lived, less and less people seem to mix with you.

Could be it's because I married a coloured person. There's a lot of people hates their guts, they do. When they walk around and they see this coloured man's got this place, another coloured man's opening that place, that's what hurts these English people —when they find that they've got one factory here, they've got a factory somewhere else, they've got a house somewhere else. They say, 'Cor blimey! Where the hell do they get the money from?!! *I* could never do that!'

Well, you see, a coloured man isn't the same as them. Say he wants to buy a building, say a sign's outside: HOUSE FOR SALE. He'll go and find the agent and the agent will say maybe '£2,500 for this property'. Well he'll have two friends who will go so much each towards a £500 deposit and they'll come and live with him in the place and the money they get from letting rooms they'll share between them. Say there was about £20 rent coming in every week. They each get so much of the £20 after paying mortgage. Maybe on £20 they'd pay off £5 to £10 a week. That's how they live. A white man couldn't do that. He couldn't go to his friends and ask for money. I couldn't get a halfpenny if I wanted it. Coloured people are different. That's why they call someone from the same country Brother. When someone comes from Bangladesh and they go in a Bangladesh restaurant, maybe that boy's come from the same village as what the Guvnor has. Well that Guvnor will say, 'Sit down and have a meal,' and he gives him two or three pound. You wouldn't find a Englishman giving two or three pound, would you? You'd be lucky if you got a cup of tea. You'd be lucky if you got a light. That's why a lot of English people don't like the coloureds—because they get on, they've got places here, they've got places all over. People wonder how they get the money. Well they all help one another. What coloured people do for their own people you wouldn't see English people do. Never.

When Basit married me in 1936 he had two houses in Plumber's Row off Commercial Road,—24 and 25—25/- a week each. We let off rooms to coloured seamen from East Pakistan, 2/- a week to sleep. We put four people in one room so that was eight bob a week for that room, another room eight bob, another room eight bob. . . . They paid 7/- a week if they wanted food. About sixteen people used to sit down for their dinner. I made a bit of meat curry or dal curry. For Sunday I got chickens. They didn't grumble. As long as they found something ready for them of a night time they was all right. Then come about ten o'clock someone would say, 'Come on, Beatty, make a cup of tea!' or 'Come on, Beatty, make a cup of coffee!' and we'd have a cup of tea or a cup of coffee, and biscuits or a piece of cake. They used to talk about their own country and write letters to their wives. Then in the morning I give them a cup of tea and bread and butter.

Basit was a fireman on a boat. He'd go away for three months to sea. Another time he'd go away for six months. During the war he went away six or seven times. The times he was back he used to go in the beershops and hold raffles for bars of chocolates. He'd roll the dice and whoever chose the number got one of the bars of chocolate he carried in his case. I worked for Mrs Needleman, No 19, Cable Street, for twenty-five shillings a week, eight till five Monday to Friday. She made ladies' coats. I did the housework and made tea for the eight girls in the workshop. Her and her husband had two married daughters, and one son that used to play in a band in Brighton. Her husband he couldn't do nothing because his body was all filled up with water. The doctor used to come down and pump all the water from his body every morning ten o'clock, and as soon as he'd had that drained he'd fill up again. He was enormous. He used to sit in the workshop in the corner. I worked for Mrs Needleman until I was two months' pregnant. Then when Derek was two weeks old I went back again and worked for her until he was five and she lost her husband and gave up the business and went to live with her son in Brighton.

I booked up to have Derek at the London Hospital and the matron sent me a letter. She said, 'We're going to send you to Bishop's Stortford.' Oh lovely place it was! A house and garden and a lovely park. I was there for two weeks when a telegram come. 'PLEASE COME HOME AT ONCE. HUSBAND VERY ILL.' So I had to come back to Plumber's Row. Basit said to me, 'Beatty, I'm in terrible pain. You've got to take me to the hospital.' So I took him to the hospital in Wapping, backwards and forwards. The matron said, 'We can't find anything wrong with your husband, Mrs Ali.' I said, 'You've got to find something. I'm going to have my baby and I can't keep bringing him here and taking him home and bringing him here again.' I said, 'Bring in a special doctor to give him a good examination.' So they brought in a German doctor. He said, 'What's the trouble, Mrs Ali?' I said, 'Well I'm very, very sorry, doctor, but I've been coming here every day. Four or five times we've come and gone home, and he's in terrible pain. Please give him a good examination, if you don't mind.' And he examined him and he found out something. He said, 'He's got to have an operation, Mrs Ali. He's got an abscess in his side.' So in the end Basit had to have an operation.

Derek was born in Bancroft Road Hospital, Mile End on the 13th November, 1937—Scorpio, I'm Sagittarius. I was in labour two hours. Went in half past eight night time and the baby was born half past ten, seven and a half pounds. I was in there ten days. Everybody at Plumber's Row except Basit went out and bought

45

presents—a little dress, a shawl. . . . They spent a lot of money on him. He was a lucky boy. We had a big party. Made rice and curry. About sixty people come. Indian music with the clappers and a guitar, and somebody brought a harmonium.

We had to move from Plumber's Row in 1939 because it was condemned. We moved to a room down in the basement of No 4, Greenfield Street and we stayed there for a few weeks till we found two rooms over a cake shop—also in Greenfield Street. Then my husband signed on another ship and went away.

One afternoon I fetched the baby from the Day Nursery in Vallance Road, put on the kettle, made him his milk, changed him, wiped his face, hands, put all nice clean clothes on him, wrapped a big shawl round him, when I heard this buzzing noise. I picked the baby up quick, I picked up my coat quick, and I'm running, running and running. I just got down to the bottom of the street when the buzz bomb come bang on the cake shop and our two rooms.

After that I slept nights in the Tilbury Shelter.

Next I took three rooms on top of a house in Yalford Street, fourteen shilling a week. I furnished them all out, took the baby to the Day Nursery every morning, went to my job with Mrs Needleman, collected the baby, come home, give the baby his food, wrapped him round, went and slept with him in the Tilbury Shelter. I don't think I was in that flat a year when I went home. It had been pouring with rain. I thought, 'No, not again!' A time bomb had fallen on the yard of a place where they made coathangers opposite my flat. (It took fourteen soldiers to dig it out. We had a whip round for them—ten pound we give.) Everything all round was demolished. Policemen and soldiers were on guard with a rope at the bottom of the road. I said to a policeman, 'I must go through, love, and get some things for the baby.' He said, 'It'll be at your own risk.' Everything in the flat was floating in water. I managed to get a few things out from the drawers—napkins, a couple of clean little jumpers, little knickers, couple of little pairs of shoes, bless him —dressed him and went to the shelter.

Well I couldn't go back to Yalford Street no more and I was walking around and walking around looking for a room till I couldn't walk no more. Then I met this woman. 'Mrs,' she said,

'You look very tired.' I said, 'Yes. I'm looking for a room.' She said, 'You can't walk around with that baby. I've got a room down the basement of my house in Umberston Street.' So I stayed with her till I found a flat in Philchurch Street, No 10, Elsie House. The landlord said, 'Yes, Mrs Ali, for ten and eight-pence a week rent and two weeks in advance'. And then I started to carry for my second baby.

One evening my husband said, 'Beatty, I'm going out for one hour, I'll come back.' I said, 'Please do come back before I'm took bad.' He said, 'All right. I'll only be one hour.' But he was gone out longer than an hour. I done all the flat out and had a bath and I'd just finished the bath, done my hair, got all nice clean clothes on when all of a sudden a pain come and I thought to myself, 'I must call somebody.' I went downstairs and I phoned the ambulance. I said, 'Please come to No 10, Elsie House, Philchurch Street, quick! I'm in labour!' and the am-bulance come and I went in the ambulance to St Andrew's Hospital.

I got there at eight thirty and Michael was born ten o'clock —the 25th October, 1942. They took me in a ward till the pains got more stronger. And the pains got more stronger and stronger and stronger, and then they took me into the maternity room ready for the baby to be born. And the baby is nearly coming into the world. And there's two doctors and there's two sisters and there's two nurses stood by. They said, 'Take your time, Mrs Ali. Take your time. It's coming.' And the head part come. Then a doctor said, 'More slowly, Mrs Ali. The body's coming now.' So I done that. He said, 'Now take your time. The body's right through now. Take your time. More careful. More careful. It's coming, Mrs Ali. It's coming.' Then all of a sudden it was all over. They took the baby. I heard the baby crying and I was all happy. I looked at it and I said, 'What a lovely little boy.' They said, 'Yes, a lovely baby, Mrs Ali. Now we've got to massage your stomach till all the afterbirth come.' Then that was all over. I was very weak. I was tired. I lay there. They washed me. They swabbed me all down. They took me into the ward and they asked me what I wanted. I said, 'I need a strong cup of tea and a piece of toast.' They said, 'All right.' So they gave me a strong cup of tea and some toast and I went to sleep.

When Michael was born I took him in the Tilbury Shelter as well as Derek. There was four thousand of us—a bunk here and a bunk and a bunk and a bunk, and them what couldn't sleep on the bunks they had a mattress here and a mattress there and a mattress there, all over the place. I was running there all the time. You'd make your food up indoors during the day. On one ration book you'd get a pound of sugar, two ounces of Stork marg and about two ounces of cooking fat and a small packet of tea and a loaf of bread . . . so many coupons to last you the whole of the week from the Welfare in Commercial Road.

I slept on top and Derek and his little brother slept underneath. Dim lights. Under the railway station. The trains used to go along the top. You could hear them. Two or three times the Germans tried to bomb the station but they didn't succeed. They was after it but they couldn't get it! Inside everyone was quiet. They didn't panic at all. There was all men with their wives and children. But Basit never come. When he was home he'd sleep in his own bed. He didn't believe in the shelter. He went to bed and hoped for the best. He said, 'If it happens, it happens, don't it?'

You went to your bunk and put your blankets down. Everybody friendly. No one argued. 'You all right, Mrs? Got plenty of room? Make yourself at home. We've got to make the most of it in here.' A man used to come round. 'You all right, love?' But that's all finished.

I took a great big bottle of hot milk for Michael wrapped in a bit of shawl. He was no trouble at all. I'd pour him his bottle of milk and he'd have it and go off to sleep till the next morning six o'clock. Then we'd gradually make our way home and wash.

Derek didn't like it. He got frightened. When he was seven and at the Dempsey Street School the headmistress said to him, 'Well, Derek,' she said, 'this war is getting worser. How would you like to be evacuated?' and she sent him to Wakefield, Durham, and he stayed there until the war was over. I went to see him once. He was staying with a nice lady with a great big back garden. Derek was making toys out of pieces of wood—little motors, little engines, little trucks. After the war she wrote me a letter, she said, 'Dear Mrs Ali, Just a few lines hoping you're all right as it leaves me the same. Your boy's getting on wonderful

48

here. He's making such a lot of toys for the children in the street and toys to take to school for the children who haven't got none. I would love to adopt him. Will you please give me your answer.' I writ back and said, 'I'm ever so sorry but I couldn't do that, love.' Then he come back and finished at the Dempsey.

We'd moved to 4, Maples Place. I was working in Della's caff, Redman's Road, washing up, cleaning, waiting—egg and chips, sausage and chips, steak and chips—and she said, 'Why don't you go after 4, Maples Place? I'll talk with the landlord. It's 17/6 a week. A three-roomed house.' So I met the landlord —a Jewish man. I said, 'Do you think I stand a chance of getting it?' He said, 'Come and have a look.' As you went in the passage there a great big room beside it. Coming up the stairs was the toilet. Coming up more stairs was another room. Coming up the stairs again, another room. He said, 'You can have this house, Mrs Ali, if you pay me four weeks' rent in advance.' There was a manhole in the passage but I said, 'All right.'

That was just before the war ended. One day a call came to Della to say a bomb had fallen in Vallance Road where Michael's Day Nursery was. I run to see if he was all right. The matron said, 'He's all right. Come and collect him when you've finished your job.' The bomb in Vallance Road was the last bomb of the war.

We stayed in Maples Place for four or five years. The landlord sent in a man. We had all the roof done and we had all the rooms done up and a new toilet put in. It cost him £250 odd pounds. But he couldn't do nothing about the manhole. Every now and again you had to get all the water out of it and throw it down the drain outside.

While we was there Basit got into trouble. A knock come at the door. A tall Englishman. 'Does a Mr Basit Ali live here?' I said, 'Yes, he's my husband.' He said, 'I don't think so.' I said, 'He is!' I showed him my marriage lines. He said, 'If my daughter don't come home tonight, you'll know what to expect.' And she didn't go home. She was seeing my husband. He'd given up the sea and he was working at that time in a tailoring factory in Aldgate pressing ladies' coats. Some nights he made out he was gambling and it wasn't gambling at all, it was seeing this machinist from the factory who was only fifteen. So her

49

father made a summons and the case come up at Arbour Square Court and from Arbour Square Court they remanded Basit in Brixton Prison for two weeks and then the case come up at the Old Bailey in Number One Court. We had a barrister, and I stood in the witness box and my husband stood in the dock and the barrister stood in the middle. I was given the Koran to swear on. 'I'm speaking the truth but nothing but the truth. Help me God.' I told the barrister, I said, 'I didn't know what was going on. What went on while I was in my job I can't tell. I can only tell what I see with my own eyes.' And the judge said, 'We're not sending your husband to prison for five years or four years or three years. We're sending him for six months.' So he done six months in Wormwood Scrubs.

Then another thing happened. One week I said, 'Derek, you've got a bike, love, go to the landlord in Bethnal Green Road and pay the rent for me. Here you are, love. Careful.' Well he put the money in the Rent Book, and when he got to the office and went in he says, 'I've come with my Mum's rent. Two week's rent.' 'Well,' said the girl, 'I'm sorry,' she said to my son, 'there's a pound short.' I went to see her and explained. I said, 'My son had the money in the Rent Book in a pocket of his trousers, and with the warmth from his leg riding the bike maybe two pound notes got stuck together.' She still said there was a pound short. I said I'd pay next time but when I told my husband he got in a temper. I said, 'No good to get in a temper, Basit. What has happened, has happened. Let bygones be bygones. Don't worry. I'll pay the pound.' No. He went up to the office and he hit the girl behind the counter. I went up and apologised to the land-lord. 'Please think it over.' He said, 'Sorry, Mrs Ali, but I'm afraid it went too far because the girl was only doing her duty when she said to your son there was a pound short.' I couldn't pacify him, and he took us to the Leonard Street Rent Tribunal and we was given one week to get out. We landed up at 29, Fenton Street down in a one room basement. If you saw the room you wouldn't put a dog in it even, but it was my room and my husband's room and a room to sleep in for my two boys.

We was at 29, Fenton Street for nearly eleven years and all the time we was there I knew that Basit had no love for me any more. There was no love, no love, the love for me was gone.

50

We went to bed and had sex if he wanted it, but that was all. He did odd jobs when it suited him—fixed a door, did a bit of painting here, decoration there—but if I didn't go to work I would starve to death and the children would starve to death. I was always running, running, running. Every morning I'd to go out and do a cleaning job. I worked very hard. When I think of what I done for that man! I stood by and helped him in every way. I looked for him like an angel. If he come home and said, 'Beatty, wash my feet!' I washed his feet. If he said, 'I've got a pain in my back' I rubbed his back. If he wanted a bath I bathed him. Love is a very funny thing. I worshipped the ground that man walked on though he never showed me one bit of appreciation.

Then one day he went to the toilet which was outside up some steps. When he was finished he turned round to shut the door and he slipped and fell on his back. He didn't think it was anything but I took him to Dr Rosen in Batty Street and said, 'My husband's got a bad back, doctor.' So he examined him and said, 'You've got to take him to the hospital, Mrs Ali,' and when they examined him they said, 'He's got a rupture. He'll have to go on the waiting list.' They give him a rupture belt to wear and then, after eighteen months when he could hardly stand up, this letter come for him to go and have this operation.

He had the operation on a Monday and on the Tuesday I went to see him. He said, 'Beatty, go home and get my clothes. I don't want to stop here.' I said, 'You can't, Basit. You've had your operation.' He said, 'I want my clothes.' And the doctor come and he said, 'We can't do anything, Mrs Ali. If he wants to go home you'll have to take him home.' And I had to go home and get the clothes and I had to help him, I had to take him home. And I had to carry him down the basement. Pouring with rain it was. Teeming with rain. He got soaked. I helped him and helped him and helped him till we got home to the basement. Then I lifted him up onto the bed, and I had to go and get Dr Rosen. I said, 'Doctor, I'm ever so sorry to worry you but my Basit has come home from this operation, he wouldn't stop in the hospital.' He said, 'No, Mrs Ali! Surely not?!' I said, 'He has, love. I'm ever so sorry but I'm afraid you'll have to come and see him.' When he come he said, 'Mr Ali, you should never have done this.' He said, 'I didn't want to stop in there. I wanted to come home. I wanted to rest.' 'Well,' said Dr Rosen, 'you could have rested in the hospital,' and Basit said, 'I don't like hospitals. I wanted to come home to be looked after properly.' Dr Rosen was numbed. Till the time come for him to have the stitches out he sent in a nurse to wash him and bathe him for two or three weeks. I had to go off, do a couple of hours' work, then run home and get a bowl of water ready for this nurse at ten o'clock to swab him. I was running to my job, coming back again—all the time. And when Dr Rosen was taking the stitches out he said, 'You ought to be ashamed of yourself, Mr Ali. This is not my job. It's the hospital's job.'

And right from the day Basit come out of the hospital he never done a regular day's work for fifteen years. He wouldn't wash a cup up, even. He wouldn't sweep the floor. For a year he wouldn't even go to the toilet—just up three stairs. He done everything in the room in a bucket. He was a lazy man who liked the bed. He got up when it suited him. If he wanted to get up at eleven o'clock he got up at eleven o'clock. Sometimes you'd come home from your job and he'd still be there. Sometimes he'd wander out and go from here and there to there, sit in a coffee shop for hours and hours, come home ten o'clock, sometimes before, and lie on the bed. He didn't want to take a job. He could have done a regular light job but he relied on me. Right from the time he had that operation he did hardly nothing till 1959 when he opened a shop in Cheshire Street—old tables and chairs and second hand clothes: shoes, jackets, jumpers— open once a week. He had a mug to look after him, didn't he? And he didn't say thank you, he didn't even say he loved me. And we'd not enough money. Derek said, 'Mum, you're a fool!' He said, 'Don't worry, Mum, You are my mother and I love you very, very much and I'm going to do a job and I'm going to help you with a few shillings.' Why should he work like that?! A kid! For a lazy lout! That was why he turned against his father and called him a yob. I don't blame him either. I wish him all the luck in the world. 'Mum,' he said, 'if you do anything he don't show any appreciation. What kind of a man is he? What kind of a father is he?' I said, 'Derek, I know. But *I* love you and Michael. You are my two boys. If anything happened to my Derek and Michael I don't know what I would do.'

So Derek worked for a man who had a shoe warehouse in Mount Terrace right until he left school for a pound a week. He used to run home from school at four o'clock, have a quick tea and run back to this warehouse and get all the shoes ready for the shops. The Guvnor used to tell him, 'Here you are, Derek. Tie up these shoes, make a pile and put them in the car. . . . Here you are, Derek. Another lot. Tie them up. In the car.' One day he said, 'Look, Derek, you're a very good boy and a very honest boy and you don't take liberties. I'll tell you what. If you'll be good to me, Derek, I'll be good to you. If you fancy any time a pair of shoes as they come in, you can always ask me, never be afraid to ask.' Derek said, 'All right.' And another time the Guvnor happened to say, 'When is it your birthday, Derek?' He said, 'I was born on the 13th of November.' There was one month to go. He said to my son, 'What would you really like me to buy you, Derek? I'd like to buy you something because I look upon you as my son.' Derek said, 'You don't need to buy me anything, but if you'd like to buy me something you buy me it, I'll be happy with whatever you want to give me.' So his birthday come. He went to see the Guvnor. There was a big parcel all done up, 'To Dear Derek. Happy Birthday. Love, Mr . . . So and so'—I forget the Guvnor's name. And Derek come home and he undone the parcel. 'Oh,' I said, 'what a lovely birthday present, Derek!' He'd bought him a suit! So Derek put it on. Oh he was so excited, bless him. He was only twelve and it was a lovely navy blue suit, and he went to work in it the next day and the Guvnor said, 'Derek, you look very nice.' Then the Guvnor's wife come to where we lived with a birthday present. She said, 'Here you are, Derek. Happy birthday! I know I'm two weeks late, but still . . .' She'd bought him a shirt and a tie and he was thrilled to pieces. He put them on the next day and he went to work in them and the suit and the Guvnor looked at him, he said, 'Oh, Derek, you're a lovely boy!'

I'll always remember the first week Derek brought home a pound. He said, 'Here you are, Mum. Me and you have half each.' I said, 'No. Give five shillings to your brother and you have the rest and, if you like, put some of it away,' which he did.

Derek was a quiet boy. Very different to Michael who was

all for sport and liked swimming and won a bronze medal for playing football against another school. He won a bronze medal—scored the winning goal and everyone cheered! He wouldn't part with that medal for all the money in the world! They liked clubs, my boys. Derek would come in, get washed, get changed, have something to eat, then he'd say, 'I'm going to the club.' Michael did the same. They never roamed the streets. They belonged to Bernard Baron's club in Batty Street, and the Brady Street Boys' Club, they belonged to that as well. Then there was a man, Mr Warren. He changed his religion to Muslim and he opened a big club in Alie Street and the boys went there. Table tennis, billiards, the pin table, and camping week-ends at Leytonstone and Epping Forest with two or three more boys in a big tent with all their food. There was no trouble. They was two good boys.

Derek when he left school wanted to be a motor mechanic so he worked in the Osborn Garage, Redchurch Street and then he went to a bigger garage at the back of Cheshire Street. Then he changed his mind and went to work in a cardboard factory in Stepney Green. One day he lost half a finger. I ran to see him at the Jewish Hospital and when I went in I started crying and Derek said, 'Don't cry, Mum. It's me that's met with the accident.' He was out of work for six months. He was only nineteen. Two men come. They wanted to know all the details about how the accident happened. They went to see the factory if the guard was in front of the machine. He got £200. Then he went into a plastic factory and after that he went to Hackney Road as an upholsterer.

Michael when he left school took a job with the Gas Company in Hackney Road. Before that a teacher come to 29 Fenton Street to find out what he was going to do. A knock come at the door. I said, 'Yes, what do you want, love?' He said, 'I've come to see, Mrs Ali.' 'Well,' I said, 'I'm Mrs Ali.' When he come in he said, 'Oh my God, Mrs Ali! How long have you been here?!!' I said, 'Nearly eleven years. I keep going to the Housing people. One week I go to Philpot Street, the next Bishop's Way, but they tell me we're lucky to have this room.' He said, 'Cor love a duck! How much are you paying?' I said, 'I'm paying thirty shillings a week.' He said, 'Don't worry, Mrs Ali. I'll do something for you. You won't be here much longer. I'll get you a flat.'

That was a Thursday. Thursday, Friday, Saturday, Sunday . . . Monday morning a letter come from Bishop's Way: 'Dear Mrs Ali, We are offering you a flat at 71, Laleham Buildings, Old Nichol Street—two bedrooms, sitting-room, kitchen, toilet, bathroom—£3-15-8 a fortnight.' We moved that day and I stayed there right until my husband run away and left me.

FIVE

The years we was at the Laleham and Basit was doing nothing he'd get up about eleven, make himself a cup of tea and eat something—bread and butter, eggs, biscuits. When I come home from work I'd cook something and then he'd go out to a coffee shop or go round to someone's house. If he brought friends back I never turned them away. 'Beatty, make everybody a cup of tea.' I'd do that and put out some biscuits, then go and cook rice and curry. Sometimes he played tapes of all the different films we went to see—Pakistani films in Old Compton Street in the West End or in Manford Street in Bethnal Green. We'd go twice a week with his tape-recorder and all the singing would go on the tape. I was just like a servant. I was his wife and I had to obey his laws. 'Take the plate away and give me more.' I couldn't even make a joke. What he done to me one time I'll never forget about. He come in and I joked with him. I laughed, I said, 'Enjoyed yourself? You look all happy tonight. I think you've been out with a bird!' He picked up a great big carving knife. I said, 'Oh don't do that, Basit! I was only joking!' He said, 'I don't like that kind of joke!' I put my hand up and—bang on —he slit the palm of my hand and I'd to run to the hospital. He was a man that you couldn't joke with. He had no time for me or the two boys. Derek he didn't like at all. He was making up his mind to go back to his own country. He happened to say to us one day, 'I can always go back to my own country and make another two boys like you. You think I worry about you two or her?!! Not on your nelly!!'

I saw in the *Evening Standard* they wanted assistants in Shell Mex. I went after the job. The Manager was Mr Smith, seven foot tall. He said, 'Are you used to canteen work, Mrs Ali?' I said 'Yes' so he said, 'I want you to be in the Veg Room taking the eyes out of the potatoes.'

There was a lot of people there that didn't like the coloureds. You could hear the talking. 'Mrs "Ali"?' I think they rumbled. One day Mr Smith called me. 'Beatty, I want you to come upstairs to be examined.' From there I was sent to St Thomas's Hospital. Everything O.K.

In the Veg Room there was one lady—she did all the washing of the carrots. There was another lady—she did all the cabbages. There was another lady doing all the cauliflowers. There was another woman doing all the parsnips. Then there was me and two girls on the sink doing the potatoes with a student putting them through the machine. There was seven great bins—four bins of potatoes for boiling and three bins for chips.

Eight o'clock you started. Eight in the morning till five, five days a week. Mr Smith, he's walking around the kitchen watching everybody working. Come nine o'clock you're called to come and have your breakfast till half past. Then you can talk, you can have your smoke. But until then no talking, the work's got to be done for twenty-nine hundred dinners. So we go, we queue up for our breakfast. We have what we like, we have tea, toast and jam and a cooked breakfast. We sit down for half an hour. We have a smoke. Half an hour is over. Finish. Back to our job till half past eleven. So half past eleven comes and we go for coffee and a buttered roll and a quarter of an hour's rest. Then we put on a clean coat and a cap ready to go on the serving. One young lady's on the pouring out of the coffees. There's two ladies on the veg and one lady on the chips. There's two chefs serving the dinners and I'm taking the dinners out from the hot-plate so people can add veg to their plates as they're walking along. Then there's another young lady, she's on the salads. There's five hundred got to be made by half past eleven—cheese salad, a sardine salad, a fruit salad, a ham salad, a spam salad and a corned beef salad. Half past eleven till two o'clock non-stop serving. From two till three, that's your dinner break. Then after one hour is gone you go back to the Veg Room and make everything nice and clean where you left off, everything's got to be cleaned down, swept up, a little bit of sawdust. And when five o'clock comes you walk along and stand in a line and you're all searched.

There's all the chefs here, there's all the kitchen staff there. Arms out. Bags in front emptied on the floor. 'Anything to take out? Your bag empty, Mrs Ali?' 'Empty.' 'You can go. Clock off.'

Two sisters was on the grill. They was there for one week but they was caught talking and was called in the office by Mr Smith. He said, 'I'm very sorry but this is a busy place. While you're doing your job you must not talk. I'm afraid you will have to go.'

One Friday I saw extra money in my pay packet. I'm thinking it must be a bonus. I come in on the Monday. Mr Smith seen me, he says, 'Mrs Ali, I don't want you to come here no more.' I said, 'Why?' He said, 'You're a very good worker but I've got too many people. I like to have a sort out now and again. I don't like to see the same people's faces too often.' I said, 'All right. Very good then, Mr Smith. Good morning.'

Mr Smith, if he saw your face too often, then you knew you'd had it.

After that I washed up for the Bank of England Luncheon Club. We could eat as much as we wanted there but we couldn't take it out. One woman coming down the stairs dropped her handbag and a packet of tea fell out. The manager took her upstairs and said, 'Here's your cards and here's your money and don't come back no more.'

Next I went after this job as a kitchen hand with the Iran Oil Company. I thought to myself, 'I'll go for it under the name I had when I was a single woman—Mrs. Webster.' There come a time that one of the other women—she was living with an African, a big dark African—she finished her work and two others working in the kitchen they were standing near to Woolworth's on the corner by Commercial Street and they see this young woman walking with this African. Oh God! The next morning when they come in—'You know *her*? She's got a black man. Has she no shame?' It comes to a big argument, a big fight. I'm thinking, 'Good job my name ain't Ali. Thank God my name is Webster.'

The one that was married to the coloured fellow had to go into the office and the one she had the argument with also went. The manager said, 'Look, I don't mind whether he's yellow, black, blue or pink! If she's a good worker, that's her business! If she's married to a coloured man, nothing to do with you! Why do you want to make an argument?!' But the young girl who was married to the coloured man she said, 'I like working here but since there's been this trouble I'm very sorry but I leave on Friday,' and she left, and I left soon after that myself because I was afraid of being shown up too.

That manager couldn't do enough for us. One Christmas he come around, he said, 'Any of you ladies like to go and see a show?' We said, 'Yes' so he said, 'All right, then,' he said, 'I'll get tickets for you to go and see Cinderella On Ice in the Strand and after that we'll go somewhere and have a big high tea.' The show was wonderful, beautiful—the scenery must have cost a lot of money. We had our tea when we come out and then we landed up in the Standard, that big hotel near Liverpool Street Station—dinner and dance till ten o'clock night-time. We all got drunk.

And the manageress, she'd a heart of gold as well. She'd put the food that was left out on the table. 'Take that home!' One evening we was all coming out of the car park into Middlesex Street where the Baths are. All of a sudden a policeman sees us with our carrier-bags full of food and he come along and said, 'What have you got in the bags?' We said, 'Nothing. Only food. We've just come from our job.' He searched us. There was one girl with only packets of tea in her bag. He said, 'I'm afraid you'll have to come back with me.' So she had to go all the way back to the canteen with him. He said to the manageress, 'One of your women's got packets of tea in her shopping bag. Does it come from here?' The manageress said, 'Let me have a look.' She said, 'No, she's bought them from outside. She goes out and does a bit of shopping of a dinner time.' He said, 'I'm very sorry to have brought her back but I thought the tea belonged to the canteen.' She said, 'No, this woman is a very honest woman. She wouldn't take a thing.' So the policeman said, 'I'm very sorry, madam.' 'Oh it's quite all right,' she said. 'I know I'm not a thief.'

I'll always remember when I was doing canteen work in Courtauld's and the Queen come to open a block of offices opposite. Someone said, 'Oh Beatty! The Queen's coming today!' and I stood there two or three hours and she just come down the flight of stairs, in the car and gone. I said, 'God Almighty! I've stood here all this time and this is the first time I've seen her in the flesh and she didn't look, never whimpered even!'

The Queen's got no time for the poor, she'd tell you that. There was the case of that young fellow Bentley and Craig, the boy who killed a policeman on a roof. Craig done twelve years in prison as he was only sixteen, but his friend Bentley got hung as he was nineteen and he said to Craig, 'Shoot!' Bentley's mother went to a solicitor, she went to the House of Lords, she wrote a letter to the Queen, and he never got off. And when his sister wanted to emigrate to Canada she couldn't because her brother got hung for murder. That mother spent pounds for her son. The Queen's not for the public, she's not for the working class. She's fed up with her job. That's why she's so anxious for the Prince of Wales to get married. She'd retire. She'd go back to Germany. It's the same with Prince Philip. He turned round and give a speech one time and he said he reckoned the English people didn't put their guts into their jobs and that's why this country is like it is today, all upside down. He said, 'The bloody English people are too blinking lazy.' He's got no time for English people. He'd tell you that if you had a talk with him. His time's more for the rich. They're very snobbish all these people.

When we moved into 71, Laleham I bought a bed and a formica table and four chairs from the furniture shop where Booth House is now, and I wheeled them home on a barrow. When Derek sat down on one of the chairs it come away in two pieces. I brought it back but the man said, 'Sorry, Mrs Ali. We can't do anything about it because you're only paying so much a week. I'm afraid you'll have to forget about it.' So all we could use was three chairs and this one was in the corner.

Then me and my son put the bed up. We chucked the old one out into the yard. But one day I was dusting behind it and I saw a little hole in the corner and a lot of dust. I called my son in, I said, 'Derek, what's that?' 'Oh Mum,' he said. 'It's wood-worm.' He said, 'I advise you to get rid of the bed or everything will get it.' So we had to chuck *that* out, and every time the man from the furniture shop come up for the money my son went to the door, he said, 'No, they're not here no more. They've moved.'

60

The man said, 'Are you sure?' Derek said, 'Yes, I'm the new owner of this flat.'

Derek when he was about twenty met this girl Sheila in the Hackney Road and they got married. They stayed at Laleham Buildings till they found a room in Stoke Newington, an attic. Sheila went down to pay the rent on a Friday and the landlady said, 'I'm sorry but you're going to have a baby, ain't you?' Sheila said, 'Yes.' 'Well I'll have to give you a week's notice 'cause I don't want no children born in my home!' So they come back and lived with me for another year and she had her first miscarriage and stayed in hospital four weeks. When she come home, my Derek picked up the *Hackney Gazette*, he said, 'Look Mum. There's two rooms and a kitchen going at 81, Shepherdess Walk, off City Road. £3 a week.' He got it. I said, 'All right, love. But if you have any more trouble and you've nowhere to go you can always come back to stay with Mum.'

Soon after, Michael married Ann and she come to live with him at 71, Laleham, and she had her first little daughter the following year in the Maternity Home in Commercial Road.

Basit started his shop on the ground floor at No 40, Cheshire Street in 1959. The shop was the first real job he done after his operation apart from the odd one to get something he wanted for himself like a pair of shoes. So I was paying £2 10/- a week rent for the shop as well as the rent for Laleham. The boys were wild.

I was working at the Kardomah in Cheapside near St Paul's, washing up, table clearing, washing up, table clearing, with an old lady. I liked every moment at the Kardomah. I liked the old lady and the old lady liked me. She was Jewish. She lived in Buxton Street off Brick Lane and her son lived in Jubilee Street —he was a taxi driver. And Veronica, the counter hand, she liked me very much and I liked her as well. Say the night before you'd washed your hair and you'd go to work the next day and you'd have your hair pinned up under your cap, when it come to dinner time or going home time she'd comb your hair out and set it in the downstairs dressing-room. She come from Ireland. A lovely face. Her friend the manageress, she was blonde. She also come from Ireland.

An Italian girl got a big bottle of Martini one time when it was her birthday. We all got drunk. Oh we had a great beano that day! A great big bottle. Oh good God Almighty! And the manageress, she made sandwiches and laid them out with cakes and glasses on this table in the basement. And we got this girl a birthday card, 'Wishing you a very happy birthday from all the staff of the Kardomah Coffee House'. A great big card 'To our dear friend. Love from all'.

She had a hump on her back. She invited me to her home one day. I saw her little daughter. She'd lost her husband. A long way it was. At the back of Wormwood Scrubs Prison. Cor blimey! What a place to live! It was visiting day as I walked by. They was all ringing the bell. 'Oh good God!' I thought. 'That brings back memories!' They send you a pass once a month. Oh it was terrible! You had two policemen standing at the side of you. The first visit you talked through glass. The next visit I sat with him in a room—still with a policeman. Couldn't give him no cigarettes, he couldn't take nothing.

Come 1964 Basit was telling me, 'Beatty, I'm going back to my country to see my mother before anything happens to her.' I turned round and I told him, I said, 'Well Basit, you've only got your mother and if anything happened to her God help *me*!' He said, 'Yes, that's right!' and a friend of his went out and bought him a ticket to East Pakistan for £135.

So Basit went on Sunday, April 14th, 1964. It was me who had to go out at six o'clock in the morning and walk up and down till I see a taxi. I got one about seven. Three men went with him—the one who bought the ticket and two others. They took three big suitcases. He never even said, 'Come to the airport with me.' He said, 'You go round to the shop,' he said, 'and see if you can make any money and pay for the rent of it.' So I had to go round to the shop and see if I could make £2-10. 'Cheerio.' Gone. Then a few weeks later Michael said, 'We're going to move soon because Ann's going to have another baby and she can't go up and down seven flights of stairs. You won't mind, will you, Mum, if you come home any time and maybe you will find us gone?' 'Well,' I said, 'you've got to look for your future, haven't you, Michael? What you want to do, love, you can do.' So I went home one night and they'd moved.

I waited eight weeks for a letter from Basit. All of a sudden one Sunday his sister's husband come into the shop with a letter written in the Bangla. I asked the landlord to read me the letter. 'All right, Beatty.' I sat down and the landlord read me the letter, he said, 'Beatty, your husband has lost his mother.' 'All right,' I say and on the Monday I send him £5-10 to make shinny. Then another letter come telling me he is married to a Bengali girl.

Well he comes back on Friday, July 29th, 1965, married to this Bengali girl and she's going to have a baby. At the Kardomah Coffee Bar Veronica said, 'Beatty, I've got a feeling something's happened in your flat today,' and when I went home there was Basit sitting in the flat. He never spoke. He was sat on one side of the table and I was on the other. I run down and bought him twenty cigarettes and laid the cigarettes on the table and a box of matches. Two hours later he said, 'I'm hungry.' I went outside and cooked—meat, rice, curry powder, chilli powder. I got a plate, washed it, put the plate on the table, put the rice on table, went back, got the curry, put that on the table, put the rice on the plate for him, the curry on the plate, went out to wash my hands. We always used to eat together, but when I come back after washing my hands the curry and the rice what I give him was already finished. Then I give him more rice and more curry but he said, 'Take it away,' and I took it away. I put the rice and the curry on the gas stove, washed up the plate, give him a glass of water. Then he said, 'I want more water,' so I gave him more water. Then he took one smoke, and no more talk after that till about eleven o'clock when he said, 'I want a cup of tea' and I went and made a cup of tea, give him that. Then he said, 'I want another cup of tea.' Then he slowly went in the bedroom and got undressed and got in the bed. Then I sat down and had a cup of tea. Then I went in the room and got undressed and got in the bed and that was that. No talk. Nothing. Then at one o'clock he said, 'I want another cup of tea.' Got out of the bed and made him another cup of tea. Then I gave him another cigarette. Then I was just going off to sleep—it must have been about three o'clock—he woke up, 'I want another cup of tea.' I got up and made him another cup of tea. And that went on for three months. I was working eight till seven, and eight till one Saturdays. Oh it was a shocking three months,

63

three months what I wouldn't like to go through again! No talk. Nothing. He didn't want to know anybody. He stayed indoors for four weeks. Everybody was asking, 'Why don't your Basit come out?' I said, 'I don't know.'

In them four weeks he only went out once—to see Michael who was living in Watney Street. The idea was, 'My new wife is going to have her first baby. How am I going to get money? I must send her money.' So he asked Michael for money and Michael said, 'All right, Dad, I'll lend you this money provided you give it to me back. I don't care if it's one year or two years so long as you give it back.' It was ten pound from the savings for the children. Basit said, 'Don't worry, Michael. I'll give it to you back.' But he never give it back.

Michael and his wife came to see him on the Sunday after at Laleham and he walked in the bedroom and shut the door. He didn't want to know nobody. My son Michael said, 'That's funny, Mum.' I said, 'I can't understand it.' Basit's granddaughter Ruth was calling, calling. She thought he went in to get something. She knocked on the door, she said, 'Grandad, ain't you coming out?' He don't answer.

His mind was different. He was different entirely. I thought to myself, 'God Almighty! After all these years and knowing I'm working from eight to seven Mondays to Fridays and eight till one Saturdays and I've never asked this man for a penny and I've paid for this and I've paid for that, why should a person treat me like this?!' I married him, I had two sons by him and he never give me money and them children had to be brought up so I had to work because in them days you couldn't run to the Assistance Board to get help. From the time I married that man—and I'm telling the truth but nothing but the truth. Help me God—I never took a penny piece from him! English wife and coloured wife don't agree—she'd have been jealous—but if he'd wanted to bring her back I'd have said, 'It won't make no difference to me, Basit. I'll be at work most of the time anyway.' I told Michael that. 'If he wants to bring her home he can.' But he never wanted to. He never brought the subject up.

August, September, October, I couldn't touch him. 'Beatty, make me a cup of tea.' I made a cup of tea, a cup of tea, a cup of tea, and unbeknownst to me he's preparing to run away. How was I to know he was going to burn the shop for the insurance and sell the flat and run away without me?

I come back from my job one day and I saw he'd bought a suitcase and two Bangladesh people were sitting and talking to him and I could understand what they were talking about, so I said to my husband, 'What? You're going back to your own country then, Basit?' 'Oh,' he said, 'Not yet, Beatty,' he said. 'I'm going to take you for a holiday.' That was the excuse. It was just to settle my mind down. 'Well,' I said, 'I could do with a good holiday, believe me!'

I'm coming home one night. In Old Nichol Street in a side-turning was a shop where they took passport photos. Basit was stood outside the building. He said, 'Beatty, come and have your passport photo took.' I said, 'All right,' went in and had it done. The owner of the shop said, 'Well, you're a lucky woman, Mrs Ali, if you're going to East Pakistan for a holiday!' 'Well,' I said, 'yes. But we'll see whether I go or not. That's up to my husband.' Anyhow I had the photo done. Then Basit went and got the form to fill in—when I was born, this that and the other. It's got to be signed by a doctor or a policeman, and all of it filled in and sent with the photo to the head office to get my passport. On the Monday morning as I was going to get this form signed Basit said, 'Forget about it. I've changed my mind. I don't want to go to my country yet. I've not got enough money to take you. Wait for two or three months.' I said, 'All right.'

Another night I'm getting off the bus after work to come through Black Lion Yard, and two men come running out of the Indian sweet shop and they called me, 'Mrs Ali! Your shop was on fire in Cheshire Street today!' I said, 'Fire?!!' They said, 'You go round and have a look, love!' When I go round, there's everybody coming out with their suitcases and all the house had been on fire and a man's been brought down a ladder on a fireman's shoulder and brought to the hospital. I said, 'Oh my God Almighty! What's happened?!' and I'm running home. My husband's sitting indoors quiet. I said, 'Basit! What's happened in the shop?!' He said, 'Keep your big mouth shut! Nothing to do with you! Mind your own business!'

What he's done is ask an Irishman from Swanfield Street to help him spray every inch of the shop with paraffin and make a big fire for £50, and he's got two other people to fill in a great big form saying the damage was so and so, so and so, so and so, making it look like plenty he's lost when there was nothing at all in the shop. He tried to claim £1000. The insurance people offered him £500. He said, 'All right. I accept that.'

He's also sold the flat for £300. 'You can look after this flat until I come back. If the landlord knocks on the door you're to say, 'I'm the owner's brother and I'm looking after it till he comes back' and that will be all right provided you're paying the rent.'

Come one Monday he's telling me he's to go to work, Tuesday he's to go to work, Wednesday he's to go to work. Thursday he's dressed up special. He's telling me, 'I've got to go and see a Guvnor in the West End for a big job and I haven't got no money.' I said, 'You're doing something else.' He said, 'Beatty, on my life, and on my sons' life I'm going to see someone.' I said, 'Tell me the truth! Don't tell me no lies! Where are you going?!' He says, 'To the West End to see a Guvnor, but I've got no money. I'll have money on Friday.' So I give him ten shillings. I say, 'I trust you like a sister to a brother,' and he says, 'I'll meet you at the Kardomah seven o'clock tonight.' I say, 'All right, Basit. I trust.' and he goes out half past five and I'm not sure and I'm crying and I'm in the flat on my own, and my son Michael used to come by the building every morning on a bike and that particular morning he dropped the bike and he jumped the seven flights of stairs and he knocked on the door and opened the door and he saw me and he said, 'Mum, are you all right? You don't look too good.' I said, 'No, Michael. I'm all right, love. Dad says he's gone to see a Guvnor and tomorrow he's giving me some money. I'm all right, Michael. Don't worry, love. Go to your job.'

I'm going out of the flat half past seven to be at my job eight o'clock. Rosie, the manageress, says to me, 'Beatty, you don't look too good to me today. What's wrong?' I told her, then I said, 'But he says he's going to meet me here seven o'clock tonight.'

Half past six she came in the kitchen where I was washing up. She said, 'Beatty, if you like, love, you can go out at a quarter to seven.' I said, 'No, Rosie. I finish seven o'clock. When you've done your job, I've done my job. We'll go out together.'

We all go downstairs to get ready to go home. 'Goodnight Rosie!' 'Goodnight Veronica!' 'Goodnight everybody!' I'm coming out from the job. I'm waiting and waiting and waiting. I asked someone the time. They said it was a quarter eight. I jumped on the bus to go to 71, Laleham Buildings. But there was no husband. There was different people in the flat and they'd changed the lock on the door. I knocked. I asked, 'What are you doing in my place?' They said, 'We paid £300 for this.' I said, '£300 for this?!! Where am I going? Oh my God! Where am I going?'

SIX

Three suitcases with a friend in 29, Bacon Street and one suitcase indoors. All Basit had to do when I was gone to work was come back, go to Bacon Street, call a taxi and away he was off by aeroplane to Sylhet! He hadn't even paid the Irishman his £50 for helping him to burn the shop! And—you know what Irishmen are like—he was wild!! He stopped me in the street one day. He asked me where Basit was. He said, 'If I knew as much as I do now, Mrs Ali, I would never have done it for him! I could have gone for a ball o' chalk for that!'

Thirty years wasted on that man for nothing! When I think of what I did for him! Who else would have gone and stood in the witness box at the Old Bailey?! A man has promised to come and meet you from your job at seven o'clock and at seven o'clock that man is already half way home and there was I stuck there like a fool from seven o'clock till a quarter to eight wondering what's happened to him!

He come back again in 1969. That time he wouldn't look at me no more. I was in the Salvation Army Hostel. He brought a young woman with him. I don't know who she was, whether she was a relation or his new wife or another wife but he lived with her in 29, Bacon Street. And he brought three boys with him. They went to Birmingham. Then when the trouble started between India and East Pakistan he decided he wanted to go back quick. He was sitting with a friend of ours, Mary, in Old Montague Street and somebody walked in and said, 'You don't look very happy, Basit.' He said, 'No, I'm looking for money to get back home. Would you like to buy this girl?' The man said, 'I wouldn't mind. How much do you want for her?' Basit

68

said, '£200' and handed her over for his fare. The Major at the hostel said, 'Mrs Ali, by God, why ever did you do it? What did you marry a man like that for?!' She said, 'I feel very, very sorry for you, Mrs Ali.'

When you've been married for thirty years and when you've got two boys by that man and they've got married and left you and when come the time for that man to run away and sell your home, that's a big loss! I sat nights in Liverpool station and after that I'd go into the toilet and have a wash and do my hair, then come back and have another sit down. Then I'd go and stand at the meths drinkers' fire in Spitalfields Market till two men come round in a motor with soup and bread between twelve and a quarter past. I'd have that and then have a walk around and a walk around or stand at the coffee stall in Commercial Street, and then I'd go back to the station and buy a ticket and go and doze off in the Waiting Room. Policeman would come in and wake you up. 'Have you got your ticket?'—and I'd show it. 'Won't be long. I'm going to work at five o'clock.' 'Oh! Sorry to worry you.'

That went on for a fortnight, then Mr Birch of the Housing said, 'You won't have to walk around any more, Mrs Ali. Here's the key to No 43, Streatley Building in Swanfield Street. Go and move in.'

But this flat was no good to me. As I went in my two feet stuck to the floor and something seemed to tell me to run out. Michael come to look. I said, 'I don't like this flat, Mickey. There's something wrong with it. When I walk around it I feel someone is walking with me.' He said, 'It's your imagination, Mum.' I said, 'No, there's definitely something wrong here.' He said, 'Forget about it, Mum, and move. Cheap rent; £2-16-8 a fortnight. What more do you want?'

So I bought lino for the floor and I bought new curtains, and Mrs Brown, the old lady downstairs, said, 'Mrs Ali, if you like you can take this big table from here and make use of it. And, here you are, there's four leather chairs.' So I said, 'Oh thanks ever so much, Mrs Brown. If you want me to do anything for you, I'll do it.' 'Yes, all right then, Mrs Ali,' she said. 'I know you won't forget me.'

That old lady couldn't walk, she had to have one of them

cradles. I used to go out and do her errands, come back, make a fire for her, clear up the ashes and do all her cleaning, then go to the pub and get her two bottles of Guinness of a night-time and sit with her. Come a time when I happened to knock on the door and I couldn't get no answer. There come another time when I saw the door was open and I called out, 'Mrs Brown! Mrs Brown! Are you all right?' Then a big fellow come to the door. 'Oh,' he said, 'you're the lady who's been looking after my Nannie!' I said, 'Yes.' 'Well,' he said, 'Come in, Beatty, because I've heard such a lot about you, and if you want anything from this flat you can take it free. I don't want any money.' I said, 'No, I must give you something.' 'No,' he said, 'because you've done so much for my grandmother. I know. When she was alive she used to talk about you, and I've always wondered who you was.' I took a polished table, a nice cloth and a lovely vase with all artificial flowers in it, and then I took a food cabinet with a drawer and a cupboard, and in this cupboard there was four pound of sugar and three pounds of Stork marg. I said, 'Oh thank you ever so much. You are a good boy and I wish you all the luck in the world. God bless you and keep you well.' He said, 'You're welcome, Beatty. Do you want anything else?' So I looked at a three piece he had there—a little settee and two small armchairs to go with it. I took them and put them in the bedroom.

The man next door to me, named Jack, used to work every night in Spitalfields Market, come home early morning and go and have breakfast with his sister that lived underneath me. It was on a Saturday morning. He'd been to have his breakfast with her and, come dinner-time, he went down again and he had something wrong with his throat. She said, 'Jack, you all right?' He said, 'Yes, I'm all right.' So he had his dinner, went upstairs, got in bed. She's calling him to go to work. 'Jack! Jack!' I asked her, 'What's wrong, love?' She said, 'I knocked and got no answer!' She phoned for his brother. The brother come. 'Jack! Jack!' They called the porter and he tried. No answer. They called the police. They had to come through my flat to jump over the wall to get into his flat. Broke in. Dead. How about that?! And Monday was to be his birthday! And if you saw the condition of the flat! Oh good God Almighty! There was no curtains to the windows which was as black as the ace of spades. There was no sheets on the mattress. All he had was a pillow, a mattress and one blanket. And he worked in Spitalfields Market! If you saw the place! I don't think it had ever been cleaned since the day he moved in there. It seemed as if a bomb had hit it. When the sister saw it she nearly dropped dead herself. She said, 'Oh good God! I never knew my Jack lived like this!' On the wall was their mother's photo. She said, 'I'm going to take that down to my place.' And that's all he had. Oh I've never seen a flat like it. Cor blimey! They took everything out that was in the flat, burned it. Crikey! He was such a smart man. Shirt. Suit. Tie. Polished shoes. And I used to think he must be living there like a king!

Well I reckon I must have been in this flat about a year and a half and a knock come to the door one Sunday morning eleven o'clock. It was my son Derek and my daughter-in-law Sheila. They both come in and all of a sudden Sheila run out. So I went after her and I said, 'What's wrong, Sheila?' 'Oh,' she said, 'I can't come up here no more to see you!' she said. I said, 'Why?!' She said, 'As I come in,' she said, 'all my inside went over!' I poured her out a cup of tea and cut a piece of cake and took them downstairs to her. 'Oh,' she said, 'I'm sorry, Mum,' she said. 'Don't think that I don't want to see you,' she said, 'but the flat's haunted,' she said, 'and the quicker you come out of it the better it will be for you!' Derek drunk his tea and then he went too. I said, 'I'll see you again,' but he no more come to this flat.

I was going out one day and I met a friend that I hadn't seen for about seven or eight years, and she was living in Cookham Buildings. 'Oh,' I said, 'hello, Mary, love! How are you getting on?' So she said, 'Oh all right, Beatty. Do you live round here then?' 'Yes,' I said, 'I only live in the Streatley.' So she said to me, 'Let's come and have a look at your flat then, Beatty!' She come upstairs and sat down and I said, 'Well what do you want? A cup of tea or coffee? Or do you want lemonade? Or do you want milk?' 'Well,' she said, 'I think I'll have orange.' So I poured her out an orange drink and she looked around. 'Oh,' she said, 'Beatty! I'm sorry,' she said, 'but I couldn't stop in your flat,' she said. 'There's something wrong with it.'

Then one morning I went into a coffee shop and ordered a cup of tea and two rounds of toast. The woman who owned it said, 'I've never seen you here before. If you don't mind, where do you live?' I said, 'I'm living in 43, Streatley Building.' 'Oh,' she said, 'you're not, are you?!' I said, 'I am.' She said, 'I don't like to tell you but somebody committed suicide in there and it's haunted!' I said, 'I've made my bed and I've got to lie on it, don't I?'

Then one night when I got back from the Kardomah, everywhere I was walking I felt as if someone was touching me on the shoulder. I thought to myself, 'There must be something wrong with this flat definitely.'

And so it went on and on, and I had no one to talk to. I used to go out to work, but when I come home of a night-time the flat was awful and nobody would come there, I never used to see people from one week's end to another. I got depressed. I lost all interest. All my interest was gone. Depression's a thing you've got to fight. You get all tensed up. You don't want to do anything. Your body's just like a bit of wood that's shaking. You feel without life, like nothing on earth. You wish you was out of this world and gone. All you can do is try to fight it with a bit of dusting or a bit of cleaning. You've got to try and forget it and get right back to where you've come from. A lot of people think nerve trouble is nothing, a load of rubbish, but it ain't. Oh no! It's far from being rubbish! It's a thing you've got to fight and fight hard. That's why a lot of people say, 'Sod it! I'm going to take an overdose!' And that's what they do. There was a young girl in the Salvation Army Hostel. Nice woman. She used to go out to work, come home, get washed, go out again of a night, come back. But she suffered with epileptic fits. And she'd been to a party one week-end. Where she was working they had a party. And she come back into the yard and knocked on the door and she said, 'May I have my tablets?' But they smelt her breath. She'd been drinking. So the Captain said, 'Very sorry, Helen, but you can't have no tablets tonight. You've been drinking.' She went hysterical. She said, 'I must have my tablets! Otherwise I can't go to sleep!' The Captain said, 'You can't. Come on. Go to your bed.' Helen started screaming and carrying on. Then she run to the toilet and shut herself in. They

72

phoned for the police. The police come with a nurse. They tried to coax her. 'Come on, Helen! Be a good girl and get to bed!' She said, 'No, I want my tablets!' They got her out and the nurse gave her an injection to put her out, and took her to the hospital over night and she come back next morning. Two or three weeks later she got up in the morning seven o'clock, got washed and dressed and went into the toilets and took an overdose. Whoever found her thought she'd fainted. But when the ambulance men come they said, 'No, she's dead.' She was about forty, and that's what she done because of depression. You'd be surprised.

When I lost my husband in 1965, that time he went back to his country, well the shock of that didn't come out in me till 1967. Delayed shock. I had a row with Michael over the flat. He said, 'Why don't you do it up nicer?' I said, 'I haven't got the money, love. When I move into another place, *then* will come the time to buy new furniture, but not at the moment.' He wanted me to buy a new side-board, new bed, new armchairs, new everything. I bought Panadol—one lot one week, another lot the next. I come home from the Kardomah coffee shop on a Friday and I just walked up and down and I saw everything coming in front of me. I'm looking at the grandchildren's photos. I'm looking at my sons' photos. I'm looking at myself and thinking what I've done for Basit and I said, 'Well, I'm going to do it!' and I took the tablets. It needed some doing, mind you, but I took them because everything come on top.

I lie there unconscious. I wake up. I'm shouting, 'Derek! Derek! Michael! Michael!' The girl upstairs hears me. She comes running down. She says, 'Mrs Ali! Mrs Ali!' I crawl to the door and open it. She says, 'My God! What's wrong?! How long have you been like this?!' 'I don't know,' I say. 'Maybe three weeks. Maybe four.' She runs for the ambulance.

The ambulance people come and they took me to Bethnal Green Road Hospital. First a doctor gave me four injections in the middle of the arm. He couldn't get the vein up. He was just like a butcher. I said, 'Aren't you *rough*?!!' Then they took me into this other room and they put me on the drip to give me Glucose—pipe up my nose and pipe in my arm. They built my body up for four weeks, then the head doctor come along and said, 'We're sending you to St Clement's to have shock treatment and see if you like that.'

I was in St Clement's one week, then a doctor called me in his office and said, 'Mrs Ali, I think we'd better start some shock treatment, Tuesdays and Fridays. How would you like that now?' 'Oh,' I said, 'anything! Do what you can!'

So Tuesday morning, nine o'clock, the nurse came. One injection. Ten o'clock she takes me in another room, lays me on the bed. Another injection. I'm right out. I don't know nothing. I'm dead. They can do what they want with me. 'Mrs Ali! Mrs Ali! Wake up! All right?' O.K. Strong cup of tea. Off the bed. Get dressed. Sit in the ward. Then come Friday, nine o'clock, injection. Took in the room. Another one and out. That went on for three months. They put a rubber thing round your head to give you electric shocks. You don't feel a thing and then you're slowly coming round and round. Then you're wide awake. A lot of people don't believe in shock treatment, but I do. It lifts the depression. I'm just on two tablets now, one Valium tablet and another yellow tablet—two in the morning, two dinner time and two of a night-time. They make you eat like a horse. Every minute I want to go and eat but I can't afford it.

They were very nice to me in St Clement's. We had cups of tea in the bed every morning. Every morning five o'clock the night nurse come round: 'A cup of tea for you' and 'a cup of tea for you.' Then she come round and give you all another cup. Then about half past six she said, 'Come along, ladies! Now get up and have a wash.' Got up and had a wash. Then you go back and get dressed, make your bed. By the time you've done that then it's time to have your breakfast seven o'clock in the sitting-room where there's all tables. We had porridge, corn-flakes, egg and bacon and baked beans and two slices of bread and butter and jam and two cups of tea. Then whoever wanted to wash up volunteered. Then about ten o'clock you'd go over to the Occupational Therapy. In there you made wicker baskets or if you didn't want to do that you could do sewing, or if you didn't want to do that you could make pin-cushions, or if you didn't want to do that you could cover coathangers round with silk. I made a tray with a big plastic picture. I had to wind cane in and out all round the edges.

74

Then you come back about half past eleven and have your dinner. Sometimes we had meat and roast potatoes and peas; after that a sweet and a cup of tea. Then we volunteered to wash up again, wipe the tables down. Then go back to the Occupational Therapy two o'clock. Come back half past three when we had our tea (bread and butter and cake and all that), clear away the table and do another lot of washing up. And then come about half past six it's your supper—nice shepherd's pie and mashed potatoes, peas, nice sweet (some days nice sponge pudding and custard, another day plain pudding with treacle on it) and then a nice cup of coffee. Then in the evenings you had your visitors. They come from seven o'clock till eight o'clock. Derek come twice, Michael twice. Then after the visitors were gone the sister come round and said, 'If any of you ladies want a hot drink, you can go out in the kitchen and make it.' If you wanted a cup of tea you could make it. Or if you wanted coffee you could make it. Or if you wanted Ovaltine you could make it. And then slowly we went to bed. We was all in bed by ten o'clock.

One day after three months the doctor called me in his office, he said, 'I think you're well able to go home now, Mrs Ali. You're looking wonderful.' I said, 'Thank you very much for helping me. I was really very bad when I come.' I went to say hello to him afterwards at the London Hospital. I went upstairs and asked if I could see him. They said, 'Yes,' and sent me along. I went to him in his office. I said, 'Hello, Doctor. How are you getting on?' He said, 'All right, Mrs Ali. How are *you* getting on?' I said, 'All right.' He said, 'You're looking marvellous.' I said, 'Yes.' He said, 'Try and keep it up.' I said, 'Are you still going to St Clement's?' He said, 'No. I was just there on a course.' He was ever so nice. A lovely man. An Indian. Two or three months later I went to see him again. The sister said, 'I'm very sorry but he can't see anybody, Mrs Ali. He's very ill. He's had a nervous breakdown.' There was a young girl there waiting to see another doctor. She come from Epsom. She weren't half in a state. The doctor questioned her husband. 'What do you think?' he said. 'Do you reckon she's getting on any good?' 'No,' he said. 'Myself I think she's getting worse.' She couldn't sit still. Her husband kept telling her to sit still. She said, 'I can't.'

I come out of St Clement's on a Friday. I'm looking at my

Rent Book. Forty-eight pound's never been paid! Oh good God! What am I going to do?! Friday, Saturday, Sunday, Monday I'm looking for a new job and I get one as a kitchen hand in a restaurant in Bethnal Green Road. I'm coming up the stairs of Streatley on the Monday seven o'clock. The door of the flat was wide open, all sawn off around the lock—along, down and along. I thought to myself, 'My God, whatever's happened?!!' I go downstairs. I see a man with a dog. He looked at me, he said, 'Mrs, what's wrong, love?' 'Oh,' I said, 'Mr, I don't know you but will you come up with me to 43, Streatley Building?! My door is wide open!' He said, 'Certainly, love.' He came up with me. 'Oh my God!' The gas meter was broken in! The electric meter was all took away from the wall! The grand-children's photos was all on the floor! The sideboard door was all broke! Oh Allah!! The tea, the sugar—everything all on the floor! The man said, 'You must call the police, love.'

The police come. They said, 'Whatever's happened here, love?!' I said, 'Don't ask *me*! I've just come out of hospital after three months and I've started work today and I'm owing £48 rent and the electric and the gas. What am I going to do?!' They said, 'Well, it's your responsibility you know, Mrs Ali. We advise you for a start to go and speak to the electric people and the gas people.'

The mess the place was in! When Barbara, the girl above, come down next morning she laughed, she said, 'You're in a right state, aren't you?!' I said, 'What are you laughing at?' She said, 'You've had a break in?' I said, 'Yes.' She said, 'Well that's funny to me because I never heard nothing yesterday and I was indoors all the time.' I said, 'Look what they've done to the door! You didn't hear the sawing?!' She said, 'No.' I said, 'Then you must have been deaf!'

I went to the electric people, I said, 'I've had a break-in but I'm willing to pay you ten shillings a week as I'm working.' An inspector come the next day. He said, 'Mrs Ali, we don't want this money every week. We want it all in a lump sum. Ten pound one shilling. If you can't find this money in two weeks we'll cut you off.'

I can't do it. I'm paying my rent and a pound a week towards the rent I'm owing. I go home one night to turn on the light but no light comes. So I'd a candle burning for six months. I saved up ten pound one shilling. I took it to the electric people. I said, 'Here's your money" and I waited in all day long for them to come and switch it on and they never come till eleven o'clock at night. For that the man wanted twenty-one shillings. I said, 'To hell with you for twenty-one shillings! I paid ten pound one shilling! Leave me alone!' I shut the door. I went to the electric people the next day. I said, 'What do you take me for? A mug? I come and paid you the money that I owe and a man's come along eleven o'clock at night-time and he's asking me for twenty-one shillings to turn on my light!' 'He never!' I said, 'Oh yes he did!' He said, 'Have I heard you telling the truth?' I said, 'Yes. I'm telling you the truth but nothing but the truth. Help me God.' He said, 'I'll see about this, Mrs Ali,' and he did. He said to the man, 'If you do that any more you'll lose your job.'

The Gas Company, they was different entirely. I said, 'Look, love, I've had a break in and what money they took from the gas meter I can't tell. You come.' The gas man come. He said, 'Don't worry, Mrs Ali. We'll put you a new box in and we'll put you on a new lock. As for the money they took, when it comes to the time to empty your meter we won't give you no money back. We'll deduct that money.' 'Oh,' I said, 'thank you ever so much!'

I became friendly with a young lady in the Gas Company. She's asking me, 'Mrs Ali, you look very upset.' I said, 'Yes. I'm living at No 43, Streatley Building. I owe £48 rent and ten pound one shilling for the electric and four pound ten in gas.' 'Well, Mrs Ali,' she said, 'would you like to come and meet me tonight when this place closes at five o'clock?' I said, 'Yes.' She took me to a healing place in Stoke Newington. A person blessed me to soothe my nerves. But I didn't like it. It made me feel more bad. People was coming in paralysed, they couldn't use their limbs. I said to the girl, 'This place is no good to me, love.' She said, 'Maybe you've got no faith in faith healing.' I said, 'I haven't.'

I went to Bonhill Street Assistance Board and showed them the Rent Book. I said, 'Look at the money I'm owing! Forty-eight quid! What am I going to do? Could you help me?' The lady said, 'Hang on. I'll see what we can do.' She come back and she said, 'All we can help you with is three pound.' She gave me the three pound and on the Tuesday the rent man come round. He said, 'Are you going to pay any back rent, Mrs Ali?' I said, 'Here. This is all the money I've got. Take three pound.' So he took it. I said, 'See you next week and I'll pay another pound off.' And he came round the following week and I give him one pound. And I'm still paying one pound and one pound and one pound. Then come a time when a big stout Welfare Officer come and he says, 'Look, Mrs Ali, can't you afford more than one pound?' I said, 'I can't. It's impossible. I've got to pay the electric money what I'm owing—ten pound one shilling. And four nine the lock. And then there's the gas meter also got to be paid.' He said, 'I know about that but I think you should pay a little bit more.' I said, 'But I haven't got any more money coming in, only the money I'm earning—eleven pound eighteen shillings a week!' So he took another seven pounds off.

For two weeks I went baby-sitting for someone next to the Naz Cinema while she was in the London Hospital to have a baby. She wanted someone to look after her little boy so I volunteered. We went round to see the mother on the Thursday afternoon from two till four, then we slowly walked back, me and the little boy. Then I went up and give him a bath, fed him, waited till the husband come home at eight o'clock. 'You can go home now, Beatty,' he said. 'I'll see you tomorrow.'

So I come down one flight of stairs. Then a little girl opened a door and said, 'Where are you going?' I said, 'I'm going home, love.' I should have turned round to walk down. Instead of that I put my foot backwards and I'm rolling and rolling and rolling and rolling. The ambulance man said it was a good job the door was closed at the bottom. Otherwise, if I'd gone onto the concrete, I could have got killed.

I had to have eight stitches. My hair had to come off. They put a bandage round my head. And my right wrist was fractured so I'd to go in plaster from the wrist up to the elbow. I was in there from half past eight night-time till half past two in the night. 'Can you walk home, Mrs Ali?' 'Yes.' So I walked home in my turban and I'd to keep that on six or seven months till my hair grew. I couldn't go out with a bald head, could I? And the plaster was on my arm for three months.

But blimey! Half past two in the night, and I walked right from the London Hospital and down Brick Lane to Swanfield Street, went upstairs, undone the door and went to bed! And it's so *dangerous* of a night-time!! The other week there was a big fight over a girl in a coffee shop in Brick Lane. The argument ended up in the street and someone got stabbed. Once these Bangladesh fellows get in a temper they won't finish, they've always got it in for you after, even though you try to settle up. They would kill you. They wouldn't think nothing of it.

But they're not as bad as the Maltese. The Maltese like all their own way. One night I'm going by to go home and there's two young women coming out of the Seven Stars with two Maltese. Well they'd been drinking with these two Maltese all night long. So they come out and they say, 'Thank you very much for the good evening we've had and the drink, we're going home now.' But one of the men said, 'Oh no you're not! You don't think we've spent our money on you for nothing! You're coming home with us! You don't take us for mugs, do you?' So I stood there. I thought to myself, 'Oh my God, I pity these two girls!' They wasn't more than twenty-five. They said, 'But we're married women!' 'I don't care about that,' said the man. 'We've spent our money and you've got to come with us whether you like it or not!' And they dragged the two girls from the Seven Stars right to where they were living and lugged them all the way up the stairs. They screamed but the men never let them go and how they got on after that I don't know.

There's an old lady who goes round feeding all the cats in Old Montague Street. Right through there she goes, then she goes right through Black Lion Yard, feeds all the cats round there, leaves all little silver cartons with meat in them, Kit-e-Kat, so much here, so much there, so much there. I hadn't seen this old lady for about two or three weeks and, funny thing, I was coming through Black Lion Yard one night and I saw her, I said, 'Oh hello, Mum. I haven't seen you for two or three weeks.' She said, 'No,' she said, 'I'm lucky,' she said, 'that I'm alive,' she said. 'You don't know what happened to me, do you?' 'No,' I said. 'Well,' she said, 'I was told to go down Hessel Street Market where there's that Bangladesh coffee shop and downstairs was two or three little kittens and the mother,' she said, 'and the Guvnor wanted me to take away the kittens. Well,' she said, 'while I was down there,' she said, 'I heard someone creeping,' she said. 'It was one of the lodgers,' she said. 'He had a great big knife in his hand. He said, "Come on!" he said, "I want to do something with you!" "Oh," I said, "you can't!" And I screamed. I belted, "Let me go!"' She was eighty-six, mind you. 'I screamed so much,' she said, 'that someone heard me in the street and they kicked the door in and come rushing down the stairs and beat this Bangladesh fellow up, and I managed to get up the stairs and out into the street. But never no more!' she said. 'I wouldn't be took like that no more!' I said to her, 'How old was he?' She said, 'He was no more than forty, if he was that.'

Last year there was another woman feeding the cats and someone went behind her and strangled her. I reckon someone must have had a grudge against her. She used to do two jobs. She used to do a part-time job in Truman's and a morning-time job in the London Hospital. This particular week-end she'd been out doing all her week-end shopping—chicken and meat and sugar and tea and milk—and they never touched anything of that, they never touched her money even. All her money what she had was in her purse *and* the rings on her fingers, so it wasn't for that she got strangled. It was in the paper. People thought it was me. I walked into a shop. They said, 'Cor blimey! You've a long life, haven't you?!' So I said, 'Why?' They said, 'We thought it was you that was strangled because you was always carrying a bag with you when you come outdoors. That photo didn't half look like you, Beatty!' 'Well,' I said, 'it wasn't me.' They got a twenty-nine year old porter for it, a porter looking after a hostel in Holborn, cleaned the dormitories out and the corridors. She was about fifty-three. They found her body in Old Montague Street.

There was another one—Gypsy Rose, stout woman, Irishwoman—she come to the hostel on a Friday night for a bed. She slept there on the Friday night. She got up Saturday morning, sat out in the yard. Someone come along and said, 'Oh Rose, could you just trim my hair for me?' So Rose said, 'Yes, have you got any scissors?' So she trimmed her hair round for her. She looked nice so I said, 'Could you trim mine?' 'Oh yes,' she said. 'I'll do yours as well if you like.' So she done mine. So we both give her a few bob.

She went out on the Saturday morning and she never come back on the Saturday night. And Sunday morning—that was the time when Alf's fish shop was open at the corner of Hopetown Street—everybody used to go there from the Salvation Army Hostel to have fish and chips and a cup of tea—while we was in there two policemen come in in plain clothes with a photo. One of them said, 'Do you know this woman?' So somebody said, 'Oh yes,' she said. 'She stayed in the hostel Friday night.' 'Well,' he said, 'she's been found murdered.'

They tried to get in contact with the people who knew her but she hadn't got nobody, so they just buried her like on a morning walk—no flowers, no nothing, just the coffin, the cloth over and you're put down and earth is put down on top of you and someone else and someone else, there might be a hundred boxes.

They're still looking for that Lord Lucan who did that other murder. They reckon he's in France now, going around with a young girl. He ain't a bad looking fellow. I think they do these things just on the spur of the moment. I can never understand it. They reckon he's got more thinner in the face and he's grown his moustache longer. I think he's giving them the run like Biggs the Train Robber.

What made 43, Streatley the worst was the young girl up above me. She used to sit in her flat all day long and then she used to go to Hackney Road Bingo Hall and come back about twelve. And you imagine trying to sleep when someone's tiddling here and tiddling there! One night—oh good God Almighty— I don't know what it was—it come down with such a BANG! 'Ooh what's that?!' My sleep was finished. I got up and smoked three cigarettes, had myself a strong cup of tea but I still couldn't rest. Then I come out of the bedroom, shut the door and I sat in this big armchair, tried to sleep. I said, 'Oh come on, let morning-time come!' Then I saw the clock—five o'clock. 'Oh,' I said, 'I'm going to get washed.' I slowly got washed, tidied up the flat, slowly got ready and I'm ready to come out. One cigarette and I shut the door and I come out and I walked all the way to the West End. I walked from Swanfield Street right to Aldgate and from Aldgate to Leadenhall Street and right through till I come to the Bank, right through Cheapside, right through and through and through till I come to Tottenham Court Road. Then I slowly made my way back. I felt wonderful. I came back through Cheapside till I come to Leadenhall Street, then something seemed to tell me, 'Beatty, bear left. You'll find something.' Went to the left, and I was walking till I come to a small little alleyway and in this alleyway was a snack bar and as you went in there was all sweets and cigarettes but further in was all cakes and sandwiches, and downstairs was a restaurant. In the window, 'Table Clearer Wanted'. So I walked in.

A young lady said, 'Yes, madam? What do you want?' I said, 'I've come for that job, love.' 'What's your name?' I said, 'Beatrice May Ali, Mrs Ali.' 'All right, Mrs Ali. Come down and I'll ask you a couple of questions.' She asked me a few questions and then she said, 'All I want you to do, Beatty, is to keep the sides nice and clean'—where the counter was fixed to the wall—'and send all the dirties down on a tray in the lift, and if we want soup you've got to call down the lift for soup, if we want scrambled egg on toast you've got to call for it. Do you think you could do that?' 'Yes, oh yes!' 'All right, love. Here you are, here's your apron. Go upstairs and start work. But, before you go up, have something to eat. What would you like? Two pieces of toast? And anything else?' I said, 'Two pieces of toast, love, and a cup of tea.' 'Yes, love. All right.'

A cup of tea and two toasts I had. Finished. 'You all right now? Like a smoke?' So I said, 'Well I wouldn't mind!' So she said, 'Well have this cigarette, love, and as soon as you've finished come upstairs.' I had half the cigarette and stubbed it out and put the other half in my pocket. I thought to myself, 'Well that'll do for later on.' Went up, cleared all off, kept all nice and clean.

Two gentlemen come in. 'What would you like, sir?' 'Well me and my friend want two tomato soups.' So I called down, 'TWO TOMATO SOUPS PLEASE!', put on the ticket '2 tomato soups', sent the lift down. Two tomato soups come up. Took them to the two gentlemen. 'Thank you very much.' Then their spoons. After they'd finished, went back. 'What else would you like, loves?' 'Two rounds of cheese sandwiches—each.' 'Anything to

82

drink? Tea? Coffee?' 'We'll have two cups of tea.' 'All right, sir.' Back again with the rounds of sandwiches. Tea. Tea. 'All right?' 'Yes, thank you very much.' Finished. Went back again. 'Want anything else?' 'No.' Then, after, they go to the counter and pay. Took away their dirties, put them on a tray that was on the side of a fixed table.

All the other customers went to the counter. They didn't want nothing from downstairs. They only just wanted sandwiches and tea or coffee.

So I kept the snack bar clean and I worked from eight till nearly four. We had half an hour for our dinner. When it was half past eleven I went down for my dinner, came back, started work again. Then about three o'clock the young lady at the counter said, 'Want a drink, Beatty? You can have a cup of tea, you know, while you're working.' So I said, 'I wouldn't mind!' So I had a cup of tea. And when it was four o'clock the manageress come up, she said, 'Well, you've done a wonderful day, Beatty. I think you're marvellous. Would you like to take anything home?' So I said, 'I don't mind, but you've got to pay for it, haven't you?' She said, 'No, love! Here you are—two bags. Walk along and help yourself! Whatever you want, you take! You're welcome to it because all these sandwiches are no good for tomorrow and all the cakes are no good for tomorrow. Take them!' So me and four women walked along. One bag full up. Filled the other bag. There's still some more left. I said to the other women, 'Do you want any of them?' They said, 'We've got enough, Beatty. You take them.' So the manageress said, 'Here you are, Beatty. Here's another bag. Take the rest!' Not like the Kardomah. You couldn't take nothing home there—only on a Saturday. But they give you a three shilling voucher every day. You could spend it at the counter or how you liked.

So I took these sandwiches and cakes. I was thinking of an old couple I knew. I came home, got off the bus and I went up these stairs, knocked on the door. I said, 'Mum, I've got sandwiches for you and some lovely cakes.' 'Oh God! Just the job, Beatty! I do feel hungry!' So she said, 'Put the kettle on, and me and you will have a cup of tea because I've got to wait for my husband to come in, he's doing a little part-time job.' So I put three cakes for her out on a saucer on the table and the rest

I put in the cupboard, and I made a cup of tea for her and a cup of tea for me. 'Oh Beatty,' she said, 'they are lovely cakes! I ain't half enjoying them!' 'Good luck to you, Mum.' She was like my own Mum. And every day I was working at that snack bar I used to take food home to her. And if I saw any children I used to say, 'Here you are, love. You want a cake? You want a cake?' I was there for six weeks, then the manageress said, 'Very sorry to lose you, Beatty, but the lady who's been away ill is coming back. Any time you're passing you can always pop in.' Ten pound clear for a five day week, eight till four. Wasn't it good?! With all your food and all them sandwiches and cakes to take away!! A shilling each they was them cakes—long and all chocolate on the top, and all inside was cream!

One day I was sitting on one of the forms by the band stand, Arnold Circus. A clergyman from Shoreditch Church come along and he sat on the same seat as me, he said, 'You look very worried, Mrs. What are you worrying about? Tell me what you're worrying about.' 'Well,' I said, 'I'm just worrying about what I've done through my life and what is happening to me now and how I've got to fight hard and all that.' He said, 'Where do you live, love?' So I said, 'In 43, Streatley Building.' He said, 'Would you mind if I come there and see your place and see what I can do for you—walk round, you know, and pray in the rooms?' I said, 'That won't make no difference. I don't think so.' He said, 'Come. Me and you go.'

And we went, and he sat down. I made him tea, give him biscuits. Oh, he sat there for two hours! After one hour I said, 'Would you like another cup of tea, sir?' 'Yes, if you don't mind.' Made him another cup of tea, give him more biscuits. 'Do you smoke?' 'No, I don't smoke.' He said, 'I will agree with you, love. It's very lonely in here on your own, isn't it?' 'Well,' I said, 'yes,' I said. 'I stay out all day and I just come home of a night to sleep.' He said, 'I don't think I'd like to be in your shoes.' I said, 'No, I don't think you would.'

1968, a year after the first break-in, they come and done me again. This time I said, 'Sod the flat! It's putting the bonkers on me! I'm not paying no more money! I'm getting away from here!' So I went to Butlin's in Oxford Street for an interview and they sent me to Bognor Regis as a chamber maid.

The staff there come from all over the world—come from Czechoslovakia, come from New Zealand, come from Australia, come from Hong Kong, Italy, Belgium. I shared a chalet with a French girl. I slept in the top bunk. She slept underneath. If you wanted to go out to the toilet . . . but I managed to keep in the bed till morning time.

At seven o'clock you used to get up, put on your dressing-gown, go and have your bath or wash, come back, make your bed, then go and have your breakfast from half past seven till half past eight. Then you went on duty till ten o'clock. Then you had a quarter of an hour's break—a cup of tea and a couple of packets of biscuits. Then you'd go back to work till twelve o'clock. Then from twelve till one was your dinner time. Then go back and finish what you had to do till half past three. Then you was free. Bingo, dancing. Oh I really enjoyed it! The girls that was down there, they was so friendly! 'Come on, Beatty! Let's go and have a couple of drinks tonight!' 'Come on, Beatty! Let's go dancing!' Or you walked out the gate and along the road and you was in the town doing your shopping. Oh it was a beautiful place! There was a swimming-pool inside. You could look through the glass and see everybody swimming around.

My job was to make the beds, clean the floor, bathroom, wash-hand basin and toilet. Twenty-six chalets I used to do.

Now this chalet number was 25, shared by two sisters. One sister was all upset when I knocked on the door one day. I said, 'What's the trouble?' She said, 'We've never slept all night!' I said, 'Why?' She said, 'Come and look at the bed!' 'Good God!' I said. 'Where did *they* come from?! These beds get changed every week—every Saturday morning two pillowslips and two sheets.' She said, 'I've got no idea,' she said.

I run down and brought the manageress up. 'There's all bugs in there! The pillowcases are smothered in them!' I said. Mr Buckley, one of the head people, had to come up. He got me to unscrew the nuts of the bunks, and all the joists was crammed up with all these bugs, and so the two sisters had to come out of that chalet and go into another one. I said, 'Maybe it was a warm night and they decided to come out. Especially as the body sleeping in the bed's hot too.' Mr Buckley said, 'Don't let this happen again, Mrs Ali, will you?' I said, 'No.'

85

When they saw the chalets, people used to say, 'These are not the chalets, are they?!!' I said, 'They are, love!' One woman said, 'For sixty guineas this! And concrete walls!' she said. 'And look at the lino!' No fitted carpet, no short mat. Nothing. Just plain lino floors. 'Good God Almighty!' she said. 'What a chalet!' she said. 'We'd never have come here if we'd known! When we sent away for the catalogue,' she said, 'it was different entirely!' 'Well.' I said, 'they have to do that to draw the attention of the people who come here!'

I believe it's all been modernised now.

I stayed there for five months till October. I loved every minute of it. I didn't want to come back. The manageress she said, 'Well, Beatty,' she said, 'I've never found anybody that's worked so hard as you in the season. I think you're a marvellous woman.'

I come back October the 6th. I went up to the Rent Office in Manford Street with ten pound of the rent that I was owing, and they refused it. The agent said, 'I'm not interested in this £10, Mrs Ali. I'm more interested in all the money which you owe. I don't want dribs and drabs. I'll give you two weeks to pay the lot.'

So when I come home one night I found a padlock on the door. I went to Michael, I said, 'Michael, they've put a padlock on my door.' He said, 'All right, Mum,' he said. 'I'll come to the agent with you.' The agent explained, he said, 'Your son could pay us all the money which you owe, Mrs Ali, but even then it's only ten to one that you'd get the flat back.' I said, 'I wouldn't like to feel that my son was going to lose all that money. Mickey, forget about it!' I said, 'I'll go and find a place somewhere else.'

And that's how I come to go into the Salvation Army Hostel —after sleeping one night at my son's.

SEVEN

I stayed in the Salvation Army Hostel for a year and a half. Then there was this girl in our dormitory and she wouldn't let anyone talk after nine. She used to shout if they did. I got so browned off I said to myself, 'I'll go down to Major Scott and I'll make out I've got somewhere else to go to.' 'Major Scott,' I said, 'I'm going to move from this place. I've got a room.' 'Well,' she said, 'if you've got a room to go to, Beatty, then good luck to you.'

But I hadn't got no room at all.

That evening six o'clock I rung the bell of the convent in Bell Lane. I said to Sister Frances, 'Have you got a bed?' 'Yes,' she said, and I stayed there for nearly five months till they closed for the summer to have their clean up.

There was fifty of us in the dormitory. At seven o'clock you go and have your wash. You come back, you get dressed, then you make your bed. From eight till half past eight that is your breakfast—cornflakes, porridge, bread and butter, jam, a mug of tea, another mug of tea. Everything finished. Then Sister Frances says, 'Who's going to volunteer to do the washing up?' I say, 'All right, I'll do the washing up, Sister Frances.' 'All right, Beatty, you wash up. . . . And who'll do the stairs?' I say I will. 'All right, Beatty, you do the stairs down after you've washed up.' So I washed up morning time and I did down the stairs. Nine o'clock we had to go out. Then six o'clock we had to be back to have our supper—a bowl of soup, bread and a sweet. Then that's finished. 'Who's going to wash up? . . . All right, Beatty.' I wash up. The time's getting on for twenty past seven: 'Ladies, all to bed!' We get undressed. Have a wash. In the bed. The lights are put out eight o'clock and you sleep. You can't get out of that bed till seven o'clock the next morning.

When you go in the Bell Lane Convent you're supposed to be penniless. So you go in to Sister Frances in her office the first morning. She fills out a form, she says, 'Mrs Ali, you're living here. You take this to the Assistance Board.' And after two or three days a Giro comes—four pound twenty-five pence for yourself for spending and she gets a ticket for four pound twenty-five pence that covers your bed and your breakfast and your supper of a night.

You can't beat the nuns. Especially Sister Frances. 'Oh,' I said, 'Sister Frances! You're such a lovely woman! God, if anything happened to you you wouldn't half be missed!' It was coming towards Christmas time. Christmas Day they queue up. 'Come on! Sit down!' Lovely roast turkey. Roast potatoes. Boiled potatoes. Peas. And more if you wanted it. Christmas pudding. Drink if you wanted it. Cheese rolls. Sweets. Biscuits and cake. The lot. Cor! And everybody got ten cigarettes. Men and women. Two hundred sit down.

St Patrick's Day—that's better still. There's dancing and a running buffet—sausage rolls and cakes and biscuits and drink and lemonade and coffee. Oh there's a real do! All Irish music. They come from Ireland these nuns. There's twenty nuns all told. And Ann on the door, she comes from Ireland as well. They're all lovely dancers. Sister Frances—what a dancer! Oh Jesus! And how old is she?! Well over eighty!! 'Come on, Beatty! Shake, rattle and roll!' And can't that Sister Frances play the piano! Oh she's a lovely lady, bless her. She said, 'Beatty, you don't half like to help in here, don't you?' I said, 'Yes. Well I like you, Sister Frances. You're my second Mum.' When finally she says to me, 'Beatty, I'm very sorry, love, but we're closing till the winter,' I didn't want to leave.

I went back to the Salvation Army Hostel but they said, 'Sorry, Mrs Ali, but we ain't got no bed.' So I'm walking around and walking around again and using Liverpool Street for six weeks. In the day I'd go in a coffee shop and have a cup of tea, and then if I saw that they needed picking up some of the cups I used to volunteer to pick them up and take them to the counter and do a bit of washing up—not for money, just for food. Then when the time come to mop the floor over I used to do all that, and then when they used to close I used to come out and have a walk around and then go over to the station and read the paper. Once when I was broke I asked someone, I said, 'I'm in a bit of difficulty. Do you think you could lend me fifty pence?' He said, 'I'll *give* you fifty pence.' So then I was able to buy my twenty-five pence ticket as usual and sit in the waiting-room till five.

And that went on for exactly six weeks and six weeks was enough. I couldn't mix with anybody. I was too frightened. There's a woman who sleeps in a doorway in Fournier Street. Mary. She's been doing it for donkey's years. I don't know how she sticks it. For a few bob in the morning she sweeps that street right from the bottom to the top, first one side and then the other, and picks up all the dirt and puts it in a sack. Then she goes round to Heneage Street where the factories are and swills out the back yards and maybe gets a few bob for that. She must have money that woman, because she stands round the coffee stall in Commercial Street till three or four o'clock in the morning and buys a cup of tea, a cup of tea, a cup of tea. Then she goes and lays down in her doorway. All the year round. She couldn't come in the Salvation Army and they wouldn't have her in the nuns'. They reckon she's running alive. And she's got ulcerated legs.

For that six weeks I couldn't find a room anywhere. Went back to the Salvation Army. 'No bed yet, Mrs Ali.' Then one Wednesday, 'Yes. You're lucky. A bed is vacant.' And I've been there ever since. They treat you just like dogs. And it's not cheap. When I first went there it cost me one pound sixteen shillings a week. Now I pay £3.20.

I took a walk down Back Church Lane and I spoke to a lady in the Welfare Office, I said, 'All these people seem to be squatting round Myrdle Street. What do you think about me?' 'Well,' she said, 'I shouldn't do that, Mrs Ali, if I was you. You wait till you get a flat. But if you find a place and you think you could stay in it all well and good. What you want to do, love, you do. If you want to wait till you get the flat you're longing for or if you want to squat, that's your business.'

So I walked around to Philchurch Street. No flats at all. Every flat barricaded up. But top end of Myrdle Street was a basement flat with the door open. I went down and made sure it was

empty. One bedroom, one sitting-room, one kitchen. I was thinking to myself, 'Here's my chance. All very nice in here. I don't
know, I think I'll take a barrow from Bacon Street to the
Salvation Army Hostel and move half my stuff from under the
bed there with some new saucepans, cups and saucers.' And that's
what I done, and I put everything in the kitchen and I covered it
over. Then I went and bought a mortice lock but, as soon as I
got back again and went down, there was these two Irishmen in
the flat. One young fellow was sweeping the floor. I said, 'My
stuff is in the kitchen!' He said, 'Consider yourself lucky it isn't
in the dustbin!' The other fellow had a leg in plaster resting on
a chair. 'Well,' I said, 'you've broken your leg,' I said. 'Maybe
you need this flat more than me. All right. I'll take away my
stuff. You are welcome.'

But the Irishmen was working for someone else because when
I go down Cheshire Street Market a week later I see a woman
from India and her three daughters. She's looking at second-
hand dresses and coats, she's asking me, 'Do you think these all
right?' 'Yes, very nice.' She says, 'Where do you live?' I say,
'I live in the Salvation Army Hostel. Where do *you* live, love?'
She tells me Myrdle Street. I says, 'Where?!!!' She says, 'You
come.' And the place she took me was the flat I wanted! Three
rooms for husband, wife and seven daughters—six great big iron
bedsteads—three iron bedsteads in the bedroom and in the
sitting-room three iron bedsteads! You couldn't move! She was
complaining. She said she didn't like the flat and it was costing
£1.50 a week towards the rates. I said, '£1.50 a week and you
don't like it!!' I was in a temper. Then her husband walked in.
'I know you,' I said. 'You once wanted to charge me £25 for
putting in two lights! In the time you've been in this country you
could have bought your own home for your own family and
you've walked over my head! To me you are rubbish!' A friend
of theirs run in, she said, 'Don't take no notice of this woman!
She's mad!' I said, 'I'm not mad! This flat belonged to me!
How could you come and walk over my head knowing the
money that you can earn! But never mind. Ama cushi, toma
cushi. You live here. I return to hostel.'

If Enoch Powell got into power he'd show you what he'd do
because he don't like the coloureds. He reckons that they've come

here to make their money and they don't give any support to this country. All their money goes home. If a person went into an Indian shop or into a Bangladesh shop and said, 'Could you help for cancer?' I bet ten to one only one in fifteen would give a penny. If a down and out man went into one of their restaurants he'd be told to get out. 'Sorry, this is a restaurant. It's not for a dosser.' Enoch Powell give a speech saying all these coloured people are coming into this country to make this country poor. He's right. The first place they go is the Assistance Board in Nelson Street to get a thirty pound Giro. And they wouldn't give you a halfpenny themselves, not if you was dying in the street! I've gone to the insurance people, I've gone to Nelson Street with them when they've been in difficulty, I've took their wives to the hospital when they're going to have a baby, and I don't think there's anyone would say, 'Beatty, come to my home for dinner.' Yes, 'I'll give you a dinner if you'll clean out my place'! But if you said No, you wouldn't do that, you couldn't get nothing! They wouldn't give you anything for nothing. Sometimes I've gone into the Nazrul Restaurant in Brick Lane and washed up, helped in the kitchen just to pass the time, have something to do so that I wouldn't be sitting around. They give me just a plate of food and one cigarette, that's all! And they're multi-millionaires! Can you imagine? They're open every morning half past six till nearly twelve o'clock of a night. They sell bhajji fulli with one of them chapati things, and that's nearly twenty-five pence—and a coffee, that's thirty pence. Then there's the kabab and a portion of onion on the plate and a coffee or a tea—that's nearly another twenty-five. Then there's Pepsi Colas. Then come dinner-time, to sit there and have a portion of rice and curry, that's sixty-five pence. And if there's four or five people sitting down, look how much that bill's going to come to! Maybe that bill would come to three or four pound because they're charging extra because you're being waited on! And all that money goes into the bank. They don't waste a penny them people. They wouldn't buy a packet of cigarettes if they could help it. And the money's going into the bank or the Post Office. At home they've got the wife and her father and mother to support, then they've to support their brothers and their own mother and father, maybe sixteen in the family back in Bangladesh. They send it through the Bangladesh Bank in Houndsditch or they trust somebody that's going to Bangladesh. I've seen people go into the Nazrul that's collecting for spastics. They say, 'No, sorry. We don't support that. We've our own family out in our own country to support.'

One of them in there's a machinist in a factory and a hajji in the mosque. He prays five times a day to Allah. 'All*ah*. All*ah*. All*ah*.' No one's allowed to touch his body but his wives. He asked me to clean his room downstairs because there was too much smell and the sanitary inspector was coming. I give the room a jolly good clean with disinfectant and change the beds, two beds for four men. I also clean the stairs and the passage. I ask him if he's happy. He asks me, 'How much?' I say, 'You give me what you like.' He give me five bob.

Nazrul—the Guvnor that's gone back to Bangladesh and wears a black jacket with gold buttons—he called me one day, he said, 'I've got something wrong with the toilet, Beatty.' The back of the toilet was all soaking wet. I lugged all the lino up, rolled it up and put it out to the dust, and I went round the corner to Truman's where they were building, I said, 'Could you give me a big pail of cement, love, if you don't mind?' 'Yes, take a pail.' Put it in, carted it back, smoothed the cement all nice round the bottom of the toilet, all round the front. Then I went and got another half a bucket and I smoothed it all the way round the back. And when that was all dry I went out and got a piece of new lino in Whitechapel. Fifteen shillings. Carried it and put that down. Didn't get the money. If you go into that toilet any time you'll see the cement hard as rock. And that is my job what I done.

This same Guvnor made trouble with me another time. He called me in his restaurant. 'Booh-by, will you come and help me upstairs because I've bought a new carpet?' We laid the carpet down, then I went down in the kitchen and helped him. I happened to go out and talk to a customer. I done no more than that. 'You fucking bastard!' he said. I lost my temper. Three Bangladesh people were sitting at a table having their food. I thought to myself, 'If they fuck me up I fucking double-fuck them up!' and I got hold of a cardboard box and slung it at them. 'There! Take that and get on with that!' The Guvnor flew after me, but I flew up some buildings and sat up there. Blimey! You do people a good turn—all day long, 'Do this and that!'—then all of a sudden they turn on you like an animal and they think that you should put up with it and take it. But not me. Sorry. I've took it for thirty years. I'm not taking it no more. And twelve years I've suffered after that and I've had to fight on. What I've been through since my husband left me is no one's business. Only I know myself.

They started on me in the Nazrul the other night. The new Guvnor with the fluffy hair said, 'You must not come in the restaurant because you are spoiling the custom. If you want to work in here you must stay in the kitchen. If you walk in the restaurant any time you're working here then I'll do something to you!' Then I turned round and told him, 'Well if that's the case then I'm going! What I was doing in here I was doing with a good heart just to pass the time and forget what's happening to me. You know what you can do with this job—you can stick it right up your arsehole!' But they don't look at it in that way. They think that if someone that I know says, 'Hello, Beatty. How are you getting on?' and I say, 'All right,' it means something else. And maybe someone else who I know says, 'Oh Booh-by, my back aches a little bit. Do you think you could give it a little rub?' Like your own brother, isn't it? And I do that just to make him feel a bit easy. This new Guvnor looks at it in a different way. I daren't go in there any more. He'd kill me. He's got an iron bar behind the counter.

I done him a job once before—from half past six in the morning till half past ten at night—because the fellow in the kitchen went to Birmingham. And three days I worked from half past six till half past ten, —half past six till half past ten, half past six the next day till half past ten, next day half past six till half past ten—so then I feel a bit tired and the next day I think I'll go in at nine o'clock. And when I went in there at nine o'clock I saw the fellow had come back from Birmingham. But this new Guvnor said, 'Why didn't you turn up at half past six this morning?' I said, 'I felt tired and then I had a feeling that this fellow was going to come back and he is back. Now I want my money. I've worked for you for three days.' He offered me fifty pence. I said, 'No, I don't want no fifty pence. If you're happy,

I'm happy—two pound ten!' And I had to make trouble with him. He wanted to hit me on the head with his iron bar. If I hadn't dodged back it would have been on my head. And in the end he give me two ten after one hour arguing with him. I said, 'I've done you a job from half past six in the morning till half past ten of a night three days and you grudge me two pound ten! Oh please! Don't take liberties! Give and take for God's sake!' Then in the end he said, 'Here you are. No more come in this restaurant. You bastard! You bastard!' Then I'm making my way to the door and I see two jugs of water—one there and one there—so I picked them up and I went whoosh, 'Now take that and get on with it!'

It's the same with Georgina. Worked in there one day eight till nine. When I think of the work I done! Christ, if I'd been up the other end I would have got five pound easy! Not bleeding fifty pence! And she turned on me like an animal! Next morning when I went in for a cup of tea, 'Go to your blackies' coffee shop! Go to the black man's caff and drink your tea! Not in here!' She said, 'If you come in here any more I'll show you what I'll do with you!' She'd beat you up. She's that kind of woman that would kill you in one minute. She wouldn't use her hands, she'd use a knife. Turkish—good crikey—or Greek or whatever she is, she's a very dangerous woman.

Eight till nine, all day I did, non stop, ten minutes only for a cup of tea and a roll. Then this lady come in. Georgina says to me, 'Now you stay in the kitchen and let this young lady carry on outside.' 'All right.' So I stopped in the kitchen. Then she asked me, she said, 'Could you do me a favour, Beatty, and go to the laundriette with my washing and ask the fellow inside if he'll put it in the machine?' But the fellow wasn't there, he'd gone out. So I went back, I said, 'I've had to put it in the machine myself, Georgina.' I went back again and it was finished. Put it in the drier. Folded it up, put it in the bag, took it back, put it in the kitchen. Right. I'm carrying on in the kitchen then Georgina came in the kitchen, she said, 'I want you to do me another favour, Beatty. I want you to go upstairs and sweep my children's room out and bring all the rubbish down. And I want you to go in my bedroom and do my bedroom and sweep it up and clean it and bring the rubbish down.' I done all that. Then

I went in the room where they keep their tea, sugar, milk—cleaned all that. Brought all the rubbish down, carried on in the kitchen, finished what was dirty in the kitchen, swilled all the yard down.

All of a sudden this lady working in the restaurant is ready to go home. So I went in the restaurant. The sink behind the counter was chock-a-block with cups and saucers! She comes into the kitchen and she says to Georgina's husband, 'I want my supper.' So I thought to myself, 'Well, I've been going on doing all this running around and I'm no better off, I've got to go in and do her work!' So I went in, I cleared all the sink off—the cups, the saucers, the spoons. I dried them, I put them on the side. I took the two buckets, emptied them, washed them all out nice and clean. I got the teapot. I emptied that and made all that nice and clean. I done all the tables down. I put the chairs on the tables. Swept the floor. Got on my hands and knees, cleaned the floor. Then her husband when it was finished he came in and he turned round and he said to me, 'You don't call that effing cleaning?! That's no good to me! Come on, give me the effing bucket and the mop, I'm going to do it myself!' I said, 'All right! Carry on!' So he done it and after he finished it he said, 'Do you think it looks better *now*?' What he wanted me to do was take the bucket and the mop and slosh all the floor with water, then go all over with the mop. Well I couldn't do that. I wouldn't have the strength to do that and keep on going over that piece of ground five and six times. I'm a woman. I'm not a man. I said, 'Blimey! I can't see no difference! I've been in the corners but you've only sloshed it all over.' He said, 'That's fucking cleaning! Not the way you've done it!' I said, 'All right.'

I was starving hungry. I was just about in. Couldn't stand up. And fifty pence, that's all he give me! Fifty pence and three cheese rolls and two cakes! I happened to be passing by one day. A man was doing the floor. I made a joke of it, I said, 'How much are you getting for that?' He said, 'One pound fifty pence an hour.' I said, 'Yeah! Up your arsehole! You'll be lucky if you get fifty pence!' And the next day when I went by she had nobody to help her, only her children.

There's rats in Georgina's—at the back of the counter where

she stands there's a great big hole. And she's got them squeaking around in the yard and all! Her sister-in-law used to work in there. She was a good woman. Say Georgina wasn't around and you went in there at the end of the day. 'Got any rolls left?' 'Yes, how many do you want? Here you are, here's four cheese ones.' That would cost you four eights—thirty-two pence. They'd only go in the dustbin. Georgina chucks them away. And she doesn't half put loads of bread in there too! If anybody had their own place they could make a lovely bread and butter pudding.

Early this year I went into the restaurant opposite the Naz cinema. The Guvnor was away in Bangladesh. Ashiq, his brother, called me upstairs, he said, 'Booh-by, would you do me a favour, love, and clean my bedroom?' I said, 'Yes, I'll do it for you because I treat you like a brother.' So I done the bedroom, made it all nice and clean, changed the bed. Then I come downstairs to the first floor where the kitchen and the restaurant is and I cleaned all round the kitchen, got rid of all the pots and pans and plates, made *it* look nice and clean. Then I went downstairs to the snack bar on the ground floor and helped clear the tables of cups and saucers and wiped the tables down.

In the meantime two bits of girls come in. They went upstairs. Where they went—whether they went up to the restaurant or whether they went up to Ashiq's room—I can't tell. What I don't see I don't know, do I? See all and say nothing. A still tongue makes a wise head.

All of a sudden two Bangladesh fellows come in. They said, 'We've come from Manchester. We'd like to see the owner.' So I said, 'All right. I'll call Ashiq.' I called Ashiq down. 'Ashiq, you're wanted!' So when he come down one of the fellows said, 'Can I have one of them girls that's gone upstairs?' Ashiq said, 'This is a restaurant. They are customers.' They said, 'No. This is different. We know different from that.' So Ashiq turned and told them to get out and then he beat me up because he thought I'd told them there was business when it wasn't me, it was someone in the street. I said, 'Ami amar! Ami amar!' but the more I was saying it the more he was squeezing my neck until I couldn't breathe and I was numbed, no word would come from my mouth, I was nearly dying. Then he beat my arms black and blue. I was all of a shake. He was calling me all the names under the sun. He took my shoes off and threw them in the road. I run. I run in the road and picked my shoes up and put them on my feet. And then I stood back and found two milk bottles and slung them at his shopdoor window, broke it. 'Good job! You fucked me! I can fuck you double!' And then I run back to the Salvation Army Hostel and had ten cigarettes to calm myself down and then I went out and had a good strong cup of tea with three sugars.

A week later the Guvnor comes back from Bangladesh. I'm not to know Ashiq's told him I've broke his window so of course I go in. I said, 'Hello, Abbe! Enjoyed your holiday?' He said, Fucking bastard! Fucking prostitute! Don't come in my restaurant! Fuck off out! Out!' 'Now don't call me those names,' I said. 'I didn't ask for that. What I did before I'm sorry.' 'I don't care! What I know I know! I tell you OUT!' I said, 'You're going to take notice, you fucking bastard! You're going to take notice!' He said, 'No!!' 'All right! You fuck me up now, then I'll fuck you up again!!' Over the road. Bang went the window again. Another thirty pound. 'Now get on with that and see what you can do! What you've done to me is *my* funeral. That's *your* funeral!!'

So I run home, didn't I?, and went in the toilet for ten minutes to smoke two cigarettes. Then when I come out I'm in the yard walking around, thinking. The door bell rings, don't it? The Guvnor's come with a police officer, with a car. 'Mrs Ali, you're wanted!' Then I'm all in hysterics, I'm all of a shake, ain't I? The Brigadier said, 'What did you break that glass for, Mrs Ali?' I said, 'Well, if anybody's causing me trouble then I do it. I've been told that when I was young. "If anybody upsets you, Beatty, you stick up for your right! Don't be shit on and let the people rub it in! If you let them make a fool of you they'll do it all the fucking more, so why don't you use your fucking brains?!" And that's what I done! He called me a bastard—and a prostitute if you don't mind! So what would *you* do?!!' 'But why did you break the window?' 'Well wouldn't you have done the same?!' I said to this Brigadier with the grey hair. 'Oh I don't *think* I would!' 'Well I think different! If anybody wants to fuck *me* up then I double-fuck *them* up! And that's that!' Then she walloped me round the face. 'Get on with that!'

Then I go in the police car. But the Guvnor didn't get in the police car. He went back to his restaurant, but I had to be took. 'Mrs Ali, you're going for a ride. All right? You'd like to have a ride?' 'All right.' So he took me to a place, a place that I'd never seen before, a Centre. Went inside. Took off my clothes. Put on a long blue bed jacket. 'Come on, Mrs Ali. What else have you got?' 'I've got nothing, love. Only this chain and cross about my neck blessed by the nuns—and my earring and my ring.' 'Take them off! It's all right, love. I'll wrap them up. Anything else?' 'Oh yes, a pair of scissors. That's all. Nothing else.' 'All right.' She put them in a bag. I thought, 'Thank God I ain't got no bloody diamonds otherwise they'd be bloody well gone and all!' 'Come, love, and have a bath. Then you'll feel much better.' I go and have a bath. 'You finished, Mrs Ali?' 'Yes.' 'Put on these nice new clothes, love. Do you want anything to eat?' 'Oh please, if you don't mind!' 'Would you like a cup of tea as well?' 'Yes, please!' They give me sausage, chips and beans, a piece of pudding and a cup of tea. 'Come in here. Let's look at your hair. Oh yes, nice clean head you've got, love! Nothing wrong. No tiddly-winks. Get on the scales. I'll see how much you weigh. Not very much!' 'How much?' 'Nine and a half stone. Sit down? Like a smoke?' 'Yes, please!' 'All right now? Happy? What you worrying about?! Don't worry! You're going for another ride now, Mrs Ali. Cheerio, love! Don't worry!' And they took me in a van to Holloway Prison, Hospital Section, two weeks on remand.

At Holloway this big coloured lady come down with a chain belt and a big bunch of keys. You should have seen the body she had! She was like a horse. Big chest, big buttocks. And her legs! Blimey! I've never seen legs like it! What a body! And a big wig she had on! Big face! Big arms! Talk about Mr Universe! Oh but I've never seen a girl with a body like that! The size of it! When I saw her she put the wind up me. I thought to myself, 'Oh good God Almighty, what have I come to!' She really frightened me. I thought, 'What have I done to deserve this?! This has learned me a lesson! I'll never do it no more! God forbid!' She said, 'Come, Mrs Ali. Don't be afraid. Don't be afraid, Mrs Ali. You're quite all right.'

Went down. I see all these girls. I thought, 'Oh my God!'
She said, 'Come and have something to eat.' I ate. She said,
'Come up in your room.' A tiny little room, bars up at the
window. 'Oh,' I said, and I'm walking around, walking around
for so many hours. Then I'm singing my song.

'Oh my Momma and Papa have gone from me for evermore.
Oh my Momma and Papa I'll always remember you by the
song you sang
When I was a baby on your knee.
But the time has come for me to think of my future
Now that you've gone from me for evermore.
Oh my Momma and Papa have gone from me for evermore
But your memory stays with me for evermore.'

And then the time was ready for the door to be unlocked
again for me to go down and have records played till tea's ready.

After tea I volunteered to do all the washing up. I done all
the washing up while I was there. And cleaning. Whatever they
wanted me to do, I'd do. There was this tall handsome coloured
woman with glasses who was in charge when it was her shift.
She had a heart of gold, she did. She liked me too much. She
said, 'Beatty,' she said, 'you're a very nice woman and I like you
very much. You don't care what you do.' I said, 'No,' I said.
'And I like you very much. You're like my sister.' That first time,
when she saw I was a bit nervous, she said, 'Mrs Ali, don't be
nervous. We're here to help you, love. Come on. Let's dance.
Make yourself happy. Jive. Jump around. Do the hokey-kokey!'
Everybody danced in this room to all different kinds of music—
the slow waltz, the foxtrot, rock and roll. They said, 'Come on,
Beatty! Let your body roll!' The fat warder, she was jolly. She
couldn't half dance! She liked to jive, she liked to swing around.
Oh I used to look forward to that more than anything! I loved
to hear the music. Beautiful records. All the latest. They had a
great big pile. There was one little coloured girl. She was only
about sixteen. Oh she was a lovely girl! Short. She used to wear
a jumper and slacks and white slippers. We had great fun, me
and her. She cried when I come away.

Every day we was woken up very early and went down to
the canteen. They opened the door and you had to go and have

a bath, or a wash if you wanted it. Went back in your room, got dressed, tidied your room, made your bed, and then come down and had something to eat. Then I volunteered to wash up. Then we went over to the Occupational Therapy. I didn't do nothing, I just walked around. Then come back and have your dinner. Washed up again. Went back in your room, exercised round your room. Then after that they unlocked your door again and you went down and had a smoke. Back to the Occupational Therapy again. Come half past three, back in your room again till it was tea-time. Then come down and had your tea. Washed up again. Had a smoke. Then back in your room again. Then down again for recreation—records and dancing. After then you went to bed.

I'd a nice room. But you couldn't go to the toilet. What you wanted to do you done in your room. I was frightened at first but I kept my body good and walked around and looked out of the window. Saw people working. Brand new place being built. Must have been a mosque for people to pray in because the people in the windows wore turbans like hajjis. The girl next to me used to scream and scream. The screams were unmerciful. She used to cry and cry until she could cry no more. 'Let me out of here! Let me out! Otherwise I'll do something! I'll strangle myself!'

The sights you saw in there! Girl would go with girl! They was all tattooed—arms, knuckles, chests. I thought to myself, 'Cor blimey!' And the love-bites they used to have! They used to kiss each other and squeeze each other. Oh good God! Lucky I had a room to myself! When it was rest time they went to their dormitory—about twenty girls in a room. Imagine that door locked what they used to get up to! Twenty Lesbians! The fights! Shocking fights they used to have! One was jealous of the other. They made each other love-beads and earrings in Occupational Therapy. They made me some. I was like Queen Mary!

Thursday was my Pay Day—half ounce of tobacco, a packet of cigarette papers and a bar of chocolate. Queued up. That tobacco had to last me from Thursday to Thursday. The girls rolled cigarettes for me. They'd put a little piece of tobacco in paper and roll it in their hand very thin. Out of an ounce of tobacco I reckon they used to make about a hundred cigarettes. They'd a knack. And they could cut down four matches out of one. I sent a letter to my son. 'Dear Michael, I'm very sorry, I'm in Holloway Prison till the case comes up on Friday week. Could you send me some tobacco?' But he never sent me no letter and he never sent me no tobacco. One of the warders gave me a brush. 'Here you are, Beatty. A nice brush.' I thought it was to keep as a souvenir. But they took it away when I went to Arbour Square Court. When that day come the Welfare Lady said, 'Well Mrs Ali, I'm going to rig you out,' and she took me in a room and she give me shoes, stockings, petticoat, dress and a coat. She said, 'You look very nice now, Mrs Ali.' And then a car come and the police took me to the court. To tell the truth I didn't want to come away. The staff was so kind, they was like mother and sister. The tall woman with glasses said, 'Beatty, I'm very, very sorry to lose you. I wish you could stay here and be with us for always. I've never found anyone like you. You're such a good girl, Beatty. You must have been a very good woman in your time. I can see it from the way you work and the way you want to do things. I think you're very, very good and, Beatty, when you go from here, I wish you all the luck in the world. You're going to the court, but don't worry. Nothing will happen to you. You'll be all right. I know that.'

The police-lady at Arbour Square she was wonderful. I was in a cell with iron bars waiting. She said, 'Mrs Ali, don't worry, love. What do you want to eat? What do you fancy? Sausages and chips and fried tomatoes, bread and butter and a cup of tea?' I said, 'I'll have steak.' She said, 'You've had that, Mrs Ali! That's a scotch mist! But you can have the sausages and chips.' I said, 'I'll have sausage, chips and beans and a cup of tea and two slices.' She said, 'You can have that,' and she give me it. Then she come back, she said, 'Want a sweet?' I said, 'Oh please! What have you got?' 'Oh,' she said, 'we've got jam tart and custard.' I said, 'Bring that along. I like jam tart.' Then she said, 'Honest to God, you ain't half enjoying yourself, Mrs Ali! Do you want another lot?' I said, 'Yes, you can bring me another lot.' Then she said, 'Do you want a smoke?' I said, 'Oh blimey, yes! Not half!' She come back with two cigarettes. 'Oh,' I said, 'I'm being treated like a lady—like the Queen!' Oh, she was so good. I must go and see her and take her something.

Michael was in the court. I told him what happened in the restaurant. He said, 'Good luck to you! They deserved it!'

I stood in the witness box. 'I swear on the Koran that I'm speaking the truth but nothing but the truth. Help me God.' 'Yes, Mrs Ali? What were you called?' 'I can't tell the word but I'll spell it—B A S T E D. But not only that, he called me a prostitute and an old slag and a streetwalker! And I'm not going to be called one of them because I'm not one of them! I've been brought up the hard way. My mother was English and my father come from Scotland. He was seven foot tall and I was told when I was young that if anything happened I'd got to stick up for myself. "You've got to stick up for yourself, Beatty. Don't let people shit on you and rub it in! You've got no one behind you, you know Beatty, when your mother and your father's gone from you for evermore!" The last words that my mother said to me was, "Goodbye Beatty and Minnie and Dorothy and Derek! I looked for you when you was babies and you've looked for me. But if anybody needs any help, Beatty and Minnie and Dorothy and Derek, never refuse!" And I've stuck to them words. If anybody needs any help I've gone out of my way to help them people because I don't want to disappoint my mother. I want to let my mother's body lay in rest—and my father—wherever they may be. God bless you, Mum. God bless you, Dad.'

The magistrate said, 'Mrs Ali, he should never have called you that.' He said, 'Dismiss the case! You can go a free woman!'

Then I got my own stuff back. 'Here's your earrings. You can put them on. And here's your chain to put around your neck. Don't worry now, Mrs Ali. It's all over. Go home. Go out and enjoy yourself! Go out and get drunk!'

Then my son and I come out. He said, 'Do you need money?' I said, 'Well you could help me, Michael, if you like.' And he gave me three pound, he said, 'Go now, love, because I've got to go back to my work. Go and have something to eat and let bygones be bygones. But if anybody says that anymore to you you come and tell me, then I will do something, I'll settle them up to stop all this argument. If they want to fuck you up, then I'll double-fuck them up!'

When it was Eide Barak, when mother meets mother and sister meets sister in the Moslem Law, the two officers in charge at Holloway—the tall one and the short fat one—sent me a Moslem card to the Salvation Army Hostel. It said, 'Dear Beatty, in remembrance of me and my friend.'

The tall one she really loved me very, very much. I decided I'd like to go and see her. I went up one morning but you couldn't go in. There was a garage and a wall and I sat on the wall and smoked from half past ten till nearly one o'clock. Then this tall warder come along with the short one, they said, 'Oh hello, Beatty!' I'd a big bunch of flowers for them and I'd spent three pounds on stuff for a young girl that I'd made friends with. She'd been in a fight and she had all her face slit. She come from Peckham and she said, 'I wish you could come and visit me, Beatty, as my mum is not well and I've got a brother that's a spastic. I wish you could come and bring me some cigarettes and some sweets.' So I asked the tall one if I could see her. She said, 'No, Beatty. You're not allowed.' So I gave them their bunch of flowers and they took them and said goodbye but I'd still this three pound worth of stuff and I didn't know really what to do with it.

All of a sudden near the bus stop a mother was coming along with three little children. I said, 'Here you are, Mum. You don't mind? Take these sweets and biscuits and cakes for your children. I wanted to see someone in Holloway but I couldn't go in.' And I give her the cigarettes. I said, 'Do you smoke?' She said, 'Yes.' I said, 'Here you are, love. Take them. You're welcome.' I had two big cakes left. She said, 'That's enough, love. Maybe you might meet someone who might need them more than me.'

Then an old lady come along. I said, 'Mum, may I ask you one question? You won't mind?' She said, 'No, love. Certainly not.' I said, 'Will you take these two cakes and have them with a cup of tea?' She said, 'Oh thank you ever so much, love. You must be very good-hearted.' I said, 'Yes. I wanted to see somebody in there but I'm not allowed. You take them. I can't carry them.'

What I've done all through my life I've never regretted it. I've done it with a good heart.

EIGHT

I met someone about four years ago. Could have married him.
Met him in a pub. I'd been to see Michael. I went in for a
lemonade. This coloured gentleman come and sit near me. 'Hello,
madam. Would you like me to buy you a drink?' 'No, I only
drink lemonade.' 'All right. I'll buy you a lemonade. You look
a nice person, you know.' 'Oh yes?' 'I'm looking for company.'
I said, 'Well I'm sorry but I'm not looking for company.' 'Do
you like coloured people?' I said, 'They're all right.' He said,
'You come my place, see if you like it. I'm not a man to muck
around. I'm a man for my home and my job and I'm looking
for company.'

Made arrangements. Went. Oh yes! Beautiful home he had
in West Ham. Very good taste in furniture. Lovely coloured
television. Lovely sideboard. Cocktail cabinet. Blimey, you should
have seen the drinks he had! There wasn't a drink you could
mention that he hadn't got. And he was only forty-five. Very
smartly dressed. From Trinidad. He'd lost his wife. He proposed,
he said, 'I want someone to live with me. There's no need for you
to work.' His wages was fifty pound a week at an engineering
works. But I said, 'No, sorry.' He said, 'Think it over.'

I met him in this pub another night and he still asked but I
said, 'No.' He said, 'I'm wasting my time, then?' I said, 'Yes
you are.' My feeling for everybody's gone. Thirty years of
marriage—that's enough. I might risk it if the right person come
along—no mucking around, someone who'd go to work and
come home and say, 'Beatty, here's money for the food for the
week and here's some money to spend on what you might need
yourself.' I want a man I can leave when he gets fed up with me.

Some men like too many fresh faces—like Mr Smith in the Iran Oil Company.

Trouble is you can't go in any of the pubs now unless you're escorted. Last Christmas someone from the hostel said, 'Come on, Beatty, I'll buy you a drink!' Went in The Frying Pan. 'Sorry, you have no escort.' Went to the pub on the corner of Old Montague Street. 'Sorry, you've got to be escorted in.' Went to the pub right down the bottom of Wentworth Street—an Irish pub. 'Sorry, you've got to be escorted in.' Went down Commercial Street. 'Sorry, you've got to be escorted in.' We landed up at the coffee stall. A coffee each and a cheese roll! When it was Old Year Out and New Year In I was in bed. I said, 'No good going out to celebrate because you're not allowed to go in any pub!' So I went to bed about ten o'clock and heard the ships from there.

I'm in Dormitory Four. All bare walls painted yellow. No pictures. I've a small suitcase and two cardboard boxes under the bed. There's a locker beside the bed like in a hospital. You can pull back the lid and put some of your stuff in there. You can't have too much because they have a turn out every now and again. Blimey, you're lucky if you find anything left!

Mothers with children have separate quarters. They've got private rooms with a wardrobe, dressing-table and chair. There's a bed for the mother and, if she's got a baby, the baby's got a cot, and, if she's got a child, the child's got a single bed. And you can go in and lock the door and come out and lock the door after you. Some are waiting for a divorce. Others had to get out of a flat because they owed rent. They're waiting till everything is sorted out. They wait three or four months. Then they go to a place called The Half Way House and when their time comes they get a flat.

One woman without a baby she was lucky, she had a single room. But she's been left two or three years now. She found a furnished flat in Wimbledom or Clapham. She wrote to the *Woman's World*, she said, 'Dear Sir, I'm just a young woman who's been living in the Salvation Army Hostel. I've been in there eight years,' she said, 'and I've enjoyed every moment of it,' she said, 'but the down and outs coming in here don't seem to worry about theirselves very much,' she said, 'they seem to let theirselves go, but I don't be bothered with them,' she said. 'And some people sit and talk with theirselves,' she said. 'Well,' she said, 'I'm different from one of them,' she said. 'I am only a young woman and I go to work every day. In the morning I do what I've got to do and feed the birds, and then I go out and do my job and come back five o'clock and just talk to my friend, that's all.' I think she got about ten guineas for that. She give it to the hostel, so I was told.

Some of the rooms have cubicles. In a cubicle there's a bed with a chest of drawers and wardrobe. All you've got to do is draw your curtain and you're inside. That's £3.50 a week. In the dormitories we pay £3.20. The rooms is swept and dusted at nine. You're not allowed back until five o'clock except on Saturday when it's two. You can sleep in a chair but you can't lay on your bed. You'd have to be nearly dying to do that.

My Old Age Pension is £11.20. Most of the pensioners hand their Pension Book in. Every week they sign it and the Brigadier goes and draws all the money. That's for their bed, their food, their clothes, then after that they get twenty pence a day spending money. I pay for my bed and keep my book and spend my money as I want. If they had my book in the office that means to say I'd have to sit there every morning for twenty pence. No fun in sitting for twenty pence, is there, knowing you've worked all your life to get that pension and you've got to sit and queue?! They don't come round and say, 'Here you are, Nan. Here's your pocket money.' You've got to sit there till it's your turn to go in. For twenty pence! Your heart would cry, wouldn't it?! And if the Brigadier has your book you've to line up for your food, and that lining up don't do you much good. When I first went in there I thought, 'Well, I'll have my food in here for a week and see how I get on.' It got me down. There was seven o'clock queuing up for breakfast till nearly quarter past when it was your turn to get yours. Then ten o'clock break for tea or coffee there was another queue up. Then when it come to twelve o'clock dinner break there was another queue up. Two o'clock is a cup of tea and a packet of biscuits—another queue up. And then it come to half past five—another queue up for your hot supper. Then eight o'clock another queue up. Imagine all them queuings all the time! All day long food. But if you'd no money they wouldn't give you a cup of tea.

There's morning prayers every morning in the canteen. The Brigadier comes in and reads from the bible and prays and gives the letters. Then every Sunday afternoon from three to four there's a service—all the chairs in lines, a ceremony all about God. If you don't go, you've got to go out in the street; either you're in the canteen or you're out in the street. What's the good of that?!

Someone sent forty tickets the other day for forty people to go to the seaside in a coach to Margate. I didn't know nothing about it till it was too late. Someone said, 'I'm going to Margate tomorrow.' 'Oh,' I said, 'I hope it keeps nice for you.' 'Yes,' she said, 'the Brigadier picked out forty of us to go and I'm one of them.' I said, 'Oh.' I wouldn't have gone anyway.

We've a coloured television which I watch of a night-time. Everybody pays two shillings a week towards the licence. At the hostel they don't give nothing away. You pay that when you pay your rent. I like Coronation Street and Upstairs, Downstairs. And there's one about a space ship. I watch the News but it's nothing now—all about politics and the Common Market. We only have the ITV. You can't switch over. This old lady puts the television on and it stays at that one station and don't change. Too many adverts. Soon as the News is finished she comes along and switches it off. I like Alvin Stardust, the pop singer. A nice looking fellow, very tall and slim, got a lovely looking face. He's a wonderful actor. Can't half sing! He sings through the mike and does actions. All the girls go mad for him. They all run on the stage. I haven't seen Englebert lately but he's nice too. And Cliff Richard is very nice. And Max Bygraves. Tom Jones is good. A girl asked him, 'Are you a single man?' He said, 'No, I'm a married man. I've got one son and I've only got one wife and I don't want no more. The wife that I've got is for ever.' But she's very plain. I think he married her when she was about sixteen. They both went to the same school and then they fell in love and then they got married. He said, 'That's the girl for me and nobody else.' When you look at him he looks a pretty fast git. But then you can't always go by their looks, can you? Diana Dors come on in a white dress to answer questions

107

the other night. What a surprise! She looked so big and plump. To see how a person can change! But Tessie O'Shea! She come on, she was full of life! And what a voice she's got! She don't look so big as she did. She's lost a lot of weight. She had a pretty frock on. A blue silk evening dress and puffy little sleeves and all her hair done. She looked great. Another night an old man was being asked questions about how he come to write songs. He was getting wild. He said, 'I think you're asking me too many questions,' he said. 'Would you like to listen to some of the songs?' So he sung three songs. Then after he sung these three songs this man asked him another question. 'Well,' he said, 'I think you're too nosy,' he said. 'You want to know too much,' he said. 'I don't like people like you.'

One night I was sitting watching the telly and it was such a nice film and all of a sudden a big bust-up started in the yard. Major Lapper said, 'Why don't you be quiet?! You're always rowing. You're a lot of old miseries. You should be peaceful and happy but you're not. You're never looking for anything but trouble.' She had the last word. After then, silence. It's always over silly little things. One woman happened to look at another one and the other had to say, 'What are you looking at?' and then, of course, it started.

The place is getting me down. Two or three of the women scream, they scream their heads off. They'll be walking around and all of a sudden they get tensed all up and the Major has to go up to them and slap them round the face. Then if you lay your purse down for one minute it'll be gone. They're mostly pensioners, walking round half dead. They get up in the morning, wash and dress, go out in the yard and that's their lot, they couldn't care less whether it's snowing or raining. I stand up and fight. I was brought up the hard way. I've worked ever since I was eight. In Old Bedford Road Hospital I helped with the patients, washed up, done cleaning. And then I was working in London right until 1969 when I went into hospital and since then I've been doing odd jobs here, odd jobs there, and doing favours for nothing. Only the other day I went into Jimmy's in Hanbury Street and he was all in a tissy-wassy and he asked me, he said, 'Beatty, do you think you could help me today?' So I cleared the tables, washed them down and washed up. Then he asked me to go to the market and get bread, the paper. Then I come back and I cleared the tables again and washed them down. Then I done his tea towels, washed them, hung them all out. Where he does the cooking was all dirty and greasy—that all had to be done. And the two boards where he does all the carving of the meat and the bacon, they was all grease so I had to steep them in hot boiling water and soda. I was there from nine till four. He give me thirty bob—one pound fifty pence—and a meal.

There's two or three of us in the hostel waiting for flats. My son Michael says, 'As soon as you get a place, Mum, let me know, won't you? You brought me up as a baby. I've got to look for you now. What you need, I will see to. Nothing second hand. I want to see new lino, new bed, new chest of drawers, new wardrobe, table, chairs, gas stove. I'll see to that for you, Mum.' But the housing people do muck you around! First it's two weeks, then it's three weeks, then four weeks, then five weeks. I've been to see the Welfare Lady in St Hilda's Club for Pensioners, Old Nichol Street. I said to her, 'Hello, love. I'm sorry to worry you again about a place to live.' She said, 'No, not at all. It's our work, Mrs Ali. I'll phone up the Housing for you.'

She spoke a long time and the message come through. 'Tell Mrs Ali she's not to worry any more. She's going to get a letter offering her a bed-sitter next week or the week after, no longer. We know Mrs Ali is anxious to move.' 'Yes,' the Welfare Lady said. 'Please do help her. She seems a very nice person and I think she'd be much happier if she was in her own place. She's beginning to get very tired of the Salvation Army Hostel.' Then she said to me, 'I think you'd be wise, Mrs Ali, to accept a bed-sitter instead of a two-roomed flat, but if you move into a bed-sitter and then you decide to change, then you can do so. But I don't think you should. You'll be better off on your own. There won't be anyone to row with, and you can go in when you like and come out when you like. When you're with someone else you've got to say when you're going somewhere, "Do you mind being on your own?" and then you don't know what's going to happen when you're out. You've got all that sort of thing to look at, Mrs Ali,' she said.

Which is true. I took a girl of about thirty-two once with me into 43, Streatley for company. I met her in a caff. She told me

she'd nowhere to go. She said, 'Ooh, I like it up here, Mrs Ali!'
I bought her food, I bought this, I bought that, I didn't charge
her anything. I said, 'You've got no money. I can keep you
because I'm working. Whatever you want I'll buy you and make
you happy and I'll lend you a few shillings till you find something.' We went out one night and had a couple of drinks, come
out, bought a fish and chip supper and cigarettes and went home.
She seemed quite happy. But come the following Monday she
said she was going out, 'I'll come back later on. Maybe five or
six tonight,' and that was that, she never come back. So it was
just a waste of time. And I spent a lot of money. I got her
another bed and all. I didn't see her till one year later. I met
her in Brick Lane. I said, 'What happened to you?' 'Oh,' she
said, 'I'm very sorry,' she said, 'but I didn't like the flat. There
was something wrong with it.' I said, 'At least you could have
told me that you didn't like it. I was worried to death seeing
you said you was going to come back at five or six.' She said,
'I made up my mind,' she said, 'that I didn't want to come back,
but I didn't like the idea of telling you in case I was to upset
you.' 'Oh well,' I said, 'forget about it.'

Anyway, the Welfare Lady says I've not to worry, I'll get a
place. Once I'm settled I may take a lodger. Or I might go
back to Butlin's. If I was a little bit younger I'd adopt a baby.
I love kiddies. I could play with them for hours.

I couldn't have stood the hostel much longer. The nuns in
Bell Lane treat people like people. They give their lives to them.
If they think they can help you with clothes they help you with
clothes. Every night you go there there's a table covered with
clothes for you to wear—coats, skirts, shoes, stockings, dresses,
petticoats, knickers, the lot. 'Help yourself!' Jumpers and all!
Blouses. You wouldn't get that in the Salvation Army Hostel.
You wouldn't get a pair of slippers. They've got them, but if
you want them you've got to buy them.

One night I went in the washroom to have a wash and all of
a sudden I saw the Brigadier come in and Joyce—a big fat
woman who pays £3.50 for a cubicle—and Blanche who's on
the staff and has a room with the job. They was bringing Mary
Woods in. She had a plaster right across her eye. The Brigadier
was saying, 'Come on! Don't be dumb lazy! Get your feet up

and get on the toilet and do what you want to do!' and they pushed her down on the toilet. No word would come from Mary Woods's mouth. I'm thinking to myself, 'If only I could help that woman I would. It will come to them when they wait long enough!' I always say, 'God waits his time but you've got to wait a long, long time!'

When I saw the condition of Mary Woods being treated like that and knowing that I daren't do anything I was choked and I went out from the hostel and made my way over to the Wimpy Bar in Bishopsgate and sat and thought how people could treat a woman like that after she's suffered all through the years that she's been in the Salvation Army Hostel. That woman has had a brain operation. She's all nerves. She walks to St Clement's every morning for Occupational Therapy and comes back every night. They don't like this Mary Woods. And once they don't like a person they've got it in for them and they worry that person to death till they've got no more strength in their body, and when they become seriously ill then they simply let them lay and rot till they're dead.

When I saw that Mary had met with another accident and the way they treated her, then I'm thinking to myself, 'Well, they call this Christianity! There's no Christianity behind that!' If you want to help a person, no matter how bad they are you've got to help that person very gently. But when Mary went over to the toilet I could see that she couldn't stand up properly. She was numbed, no words would come from her mouth and she was shaking from head to foot. Then I'm looking, I'm thinking, 'Oh my God, if *I* could only help her!' If I could have helped that person it wouldn't have needed three people. I could have done it on my own. Because I've helped Mary Woods many and many a time when she's come into the washroom. She's always said to me, 'Hello, Beatty. How are you getting on?' And I've always said to her, 'Hello, Mary. How are you today?' 'I'm all right, Beatty.' And she's stood at that sink with the soap and flannel and I've said to her many and many a time, 'Mary, don't worry, love. I'll give you a wash.' And I've washed Mary Woods's face and hands and I've wiped her face and hands, and she's given me such a wonderful smile and she's said to me, 'Thank you ever so much, Beatty,' she's said. 'You are a nice woman, Beatty, and

I like you very much.' And then I've turned round to Mary Woods, I've said, 'Well I like you also, Mary, because you put me in mind of my Mum. God bless you, Mary.'

I remember the time when I was in my bed and something seemed to tell me, 'Beatty, get up quickly! There's something happened somewhere!' and I jumped from the bed and run in the bathroom and had a bath and I prayed and prayed and I got dressed and very slowly I'm making my way to the door to get out into the street. I knew something had happened to my son's wife Ann because she was having a baby. Kitty, the night attendant, turned round and said, 'Mrs Ali, where are you going?' I said, 'I want to go out from here to see my daughter.' She said, 'To hell with your daughter!' I said, 'To hell with you and all!' She said, 'To hell with your daughter and to hell with you as well!' I said, 'Well it will come home to you one day! God takes his time, but very slowly! Go to bloody fire!'

And something *did* happen to her! She sprained her foot and she showed everybody her foot. 'Oh I've sprained my foot!' Then I'm thinking, 'Fucking good job! You wished my daughter in hell *and* me, and God has paid you back the penalty for what you said! You're a fucking bitch. You've sprained your fucking ankle. I hope you break your fucking neck!'

The same thing happened with Major Lapper. I was queuing up in the canteen for a cup of tea. She looked at me and she said, 'What do you want?' I said, 'I only want a cup of tea, Major, if you don't mind—please.' 'Don't you want nothing to eat?' I said, 'No.' 'Well no tea without food!' I said, 'Well maybe you might need a cup of tea more than I do one day but God takes his time! You call yourself a Christian! There's no Christianity in here! If it wasn't for the likes of us you wouldn't be wanted here!' So she turned round and said, 'You people are making me sick! I'm fed up with the job. I'd be more happy if I was in a factory and living with my mother!' Then I said, 'What about these people in here?! We're being treated like animals, not like human beings!' She said, 'I couldn't care less!' So I said, 'Well why are you a Salvation Army woman?!' Then she turned round and said, 'That's *my* business!' 'Oh well, is it your business?' I said. Then I turned round and said, 'Well, if you don't like us here why *don't* you change your job?! Go and work in a factory!' She said, 'I'd be better off!! I'd have my wages every week instead of looking after you filthy rotten people, people that are making me sick and ill from the filth and the work that I have to do—bathing them and turning out this cupboard and turning out that cupboard when people hoard this up and that up instead of getting rid of it!' 'But,' I said, 'that's nothing! I've looked after two hundred people in Old Bedford Road Hospital—me and my two sisters and my brother from the ages of eight, nine, ten and eleven! We was happy! We thought every minute we was doing a good job helping them that needed us more than we needed them!'

Everybody who is brought into the world you've got to help that person. God is good to them that's good to others, but if you're no good to anybody then you will pay the penalty when the time comes for you. And the Major she got bad legs! She had them all done up, couldn't walk! It always comes home to them that wait, but God takes his time very slowly in years to come. It don't come at the time but it comes years later.

One night I was sitting and I thought to myself, 'Oh, I don't know! I'll go out for a walk round!' So I made my way from Hopetown Street to Commercial Street. Walking along I took out a cigarette. All of a sudden I saw a young couple and it was the fellow that spoke, he said, 'Excuse me, madam,' he said, 'but we've hitched and hiked all the way from Coventry, me and my wife, and my wife's very sick.' And by gum didn't she look sick! He said, 'Do you know where we could stay the night?' I said, 'Yes. Come, I'll take you.' 'But,' he said, 'we've got no money.' 'Oh you'll be all right,' I said. 'Come on!'

So I took her to the nuns' place, rung the bell. Sister Frances come to the door, she said, 'Yes, Mrs Ali? What's the matter?' 'Well,' I said, 'I found this couple in Commercial Street and she's a very sick girl. She's on special tablets.' So Sister Frances said, 'Come in!' and he said, 'Can I come in too?' 'Oh no,' she said. 'This is only for women, sir. But round the corner's for men.' So he said to his wife, 'Do you think you'll be all right, love?' 'Yes,' she said. He said to her, 'Are you sure?' She said, 'Yes,' so he said to Sister Frances, 'Give her two of these tablets before she goes to bed.' Sister Frances said, 'All right. I understand. One of our nuns is a doctor.' So his wife went in. He said, 'Just a minute, sister!' he said. 'If I can't get in round the men's side what can I do?' 'Well you go round the Salvation Army Hostel in Middlesex Street.' I said, 'Now come!' and we went round the corner.

I rung the bell. I said to the man at the door, 'Have you got any empty beds?' He said, 'No, love. We're full right up. Go to Middlesex Street.' So we went to Middlesex Street. I asked the man at the door, I said, 'Excuse me, mister, but this young fellow wants to stay the night and he's got no money.' 'Well,' he said, 'he can't stop now, love. He would have to sit down in the basement and watch the television till eleven o'clock.' So I said to him, 'Would you mind sitting downstairs looking at television till eleven o'clock?' He said, 'But I'm hungry! I've never ate all day!' So the man said, 'Have a walk round, and then come back at eleven o'clock.' I said to the fellow. 'All right, then. You come with me and I'll buy you something in the Wimpy.'

So we went into the Wimpy and I bought him a tea, three slices of bread and butter and a portion of chips. I had twenty cigarettes. I thought, 'Well thank God for that! I've got a cigarette!' So I took him his chips, his three slices and his cup of tea. He had that. I said to him, 'Would you like another cup of tea, love?' He said, 'Oh yes please, if you don't mind!' So I took him another cup of tea, paid the bill. He said, 'Have you got a smoke?' I said, 'Yes.' So I opened my packet and I gave him a cigarette. Then the time was getting on towards quarter past ten. I said, 'I'm in the Salvation Army Hostel, love, and I've got to be in by half past ten. I'll slowly walk back with you and all you've got to do, love, is to sit there and watch the telly till eleven o'clock.' 'But,' he said, 'how will I be able to find my wife? She don't know this place.' I said, 'Well—I'll tell you what—tomorrow morning, on my word of honour—I won't let you down—I'll meet you here at eight o'clock because in the nuns' place you get called up at seven o'clock. You make your bed, you have your wash, and you come down at eight o'clock and you have your breakfast. You're not allowed out till you've had something to eat.' I said, 'I'll be fair with you, I'll come and meet you here at eight o'clock in the morning and then me and you will wait for your wife. All right?' 'Yes.' Then he said, 'Could you give me a few cigarettes?' I said, 'All right. Here you are. Four cigarettes. You all right now?' 'Yes, love. Thank you ever so much. Good night. God bless.' He went down the basement.

So I got up about half past six next morning and I went and had a wash and slowly walked back, made my bed, slowly got dressed and I come out about half past seven, slowly made my way to Middlesex Street and I asked at the door, I said, 'Is the young fellow gone yet?' He said, 'No, I'll call him.' He come out. 'Oh Mrs!' he said, 'I wouldn't like to live in that place for all the money in the world!' he said. 'You know what?' he said. 'When I saw the state of the men,' he said, 'I got frightened! I couldn't sleep. I've been awake all night,' he said. He said, 'I couldn't have another night like that!' I said, 'Don't worry, love. Come. We'll meet your wife now.' So we went to the nuns. Ann on the door said, 'She's having her breakfast. You don't mind waiting?' I said, 'No. All right, Ann.' So we waited and waited till nearly twenty to nine and she come out. So I said to her husband, 'Do you want anything?' He said, 'I wouldn't mind a cup of tea.' So I took them to Stan's in Osborn Street and I bought her a cup of tea and I bought him a cup of tea. I said, 'Where are you going to now?' He said, 'To Victoria. There's a place there where people will help us.' I said, 'Are you sure?' He said, 'Yes.' He said to me, 'Would you like my wife's photo—just for a souvenir?' And he gave me a little photo of his wife. I said, 'Are you *sure* you're going to be all right? You've got your fare to go on the bus?' He said, 'No.' I said, 'Well here you are. Here's thirty pence.' So I gave him the thirty pence and a last cigarette, I said, 'God bless you. That's all I can do for you.' He said, 'Don't worry, love. As soon as we get help at Victoria we're going back to where we come from. We don't like London,' he said. 'No more hostels.'

He was twenty and she was only eighteen.

I was sitting in the hostel another night when something seemed to tell me, 'Beatty, why don't you go out and have a walk round? It'll do you good.' So I'm making my way through Fashion Street and making my way to Bell Lane when all of a sudden I saw an old man sitting on some bricks and he was shivering. So I said to him, 'Hello, Dad! What's wrong?' He said, 'I can't get in here.' I said, 'Where?' He said, 'This door.

I've been banging and banging and my sister won't answer.'
Then he started to call out his sister's name. I said, 'I don't think
she's there, Dad.' Then *I* banged and banged and called out her
name. But no answer. Then I said, 'Dad, must be something's
happened! What *did* happen between you and your sister?' He
said, 'She's got fed up with me because I wander from my bedroom into the kitchen to make myself a cup of tea. She shouts,
"What are you doing?!" "Well I'm only making a cup of tea!"
"You're a nuisance! I wish you'd clear out!" '

And that's what happened. She chucked him out. I took pity
on him, I said, 'Come, Dad. I'll buy you something to eat.' He
said, 'Oh that's good because I'm very, very hungry, I've never
had no food for three days.' 'Oh,' I said, '*Dad*! I'm ever so sorry
but come!' and I got hold of his hand and we made our way to
Liverpool Street Station. He said, 'Where are you taking me?'
I said, 'I'll take you right down where the men go and have a
wash, love, and I'll give you money for soap, and I'll give you
the money for a towel, then you can go to the toilet, then you
can wash your hands and wash your face and then you can
come up and we'll go to the Wimpy and I'll buy you something
to eat to make you happy. All right, Dad? You like that?' 'Oh
yes, Mum. I like that very, very much. You are so kind!' I said,
'You are my second Dad.'

So he come up and we went to the Wimpy. He said, 'Oh, it's
lovely and warm in here. Have you got a cigarette?' I said,
'Course, Dad. I'll give you a cigarette. Here you are, Dad.' So
I put it in his mouth and I give him a light. 'Oh,' he said, 'thank
you ever so much,' he said. 'It's nice to meet nice people when
you need someone and you're down and out.' I said, 'Yes, Dad.'
So I went to the counter and I ordered him a big portion of
chips and a coffee and a buttered roll and I took it to him and
I laid it down and I said, 'Here you are, Dad. Here's a fork
to eat your chips with. Here's your coffee and here's your
buttered roll.' And I saw him put a chip to his mouth, and he
looked at me and he smiled, he give me such a lovely smile, and
he said, 'Oh thank you ever so much, love for what you are
doing for me.' I said, 'I've been through what you're going
through. It's come to me many and many a time. Any time I
see you, Dad, I'll never forget you. I'll always treat you.' And I

looked after him for nearly one week and a half. He didn't want to go in a hostel. He was eighty-eight. He come years and years ago from Russia.

One night something seemed to tell me to go and look for him again. He was in a street. I don't know the name but you go right down Bell Lane and round the corner and along and round another corner and down. And I found him an armchair and I sat him in this armchair and he said, 'Oh I feel lovely now, Mum. Thank you ever so much.' I said, 'Well I must go now or I'll be too late for the hostel.'

Come another night I took him and give him money to go and have a nice wash in Liverpool Street Station, and all of a sudden a gentleman come along with a sack and I saw him put the sack near a dustbin and walk away. I called, I said, 'Mister! You've left your bag!' He said, 'I don't want it, love. I've left it for somebody that may need it more than me.'

So when Dad come up I said, 'Oh Dad, I've got something for you. Maybe it will fit you. It's a suit, Dad. Go down into the toilet again and try it on!' So he took his dirty trousers off and he come up. He said, 'Look, Mum! It fits me nice, don't it?!' 'Oh,' I said, 'you look lovely. You *do* look nice!' It was very dark green, with a little pin-stripe in it, and the coat had three gold buttons down one side and three gold buttons down the other side, double breasted. He asked me what to do with his old trousers. I said, 'Give them to me!' and I put them in the dustbin and then I took him to the Wimpy to buy him more chips and rolls and coffee. There was another coat I was carrying from the sack, and we met someone in a ragged old coat and I said to him, 'Here's a coat if it'll fit you.' He said, 'I could do with a coat, love. I'll take this one off and I'll try that one on. . . . Oh,' he said, 'it fits me lovely! Thank you ever so much!' Then he asked me, he said, 'Have you got a cigarette?' I said, 'Yes, here you are. Here's a couple of cigarettes,' and I give him a light and I said, 'And here you are, here's ten new pence. You go and have a nice cup of tea.' He said, 'Thank you ever so much.'

I've bought a bedside cabinet in Hanbury Street for when I move—£2.50. The Brigadier's keeping it in the workshop. I'm going to get a flat—one big bedroom and a kitchen and toilet and bathroom—on the Boundary Estate. My son was on about it last week. He's still a bit off-handed. He's not the boy he was before. About a year and a half ago we had some trouble because I couldn't find a room. Ann thought I was too lazy to look for one. One thing led to another. She screamed and I run out of the house and she flew after me along Commercial Road. Michael had to get hold of her and pull her back near the bus stop. That's why they never sent me no Christmas card, no money, no nothing, wouldn't help me.

It started like this. He said to me, 'Haven't you found a place yet?' I said, 'No.' So then she turned round and said, 'I think you're too damned lazy to look for one.' I said, 'Well no one's tried more hard than me!' She said, 'I don't believe you. You're a liar.' I said, 'But you can't just walk out now, Ann, and get a room.' I said, 'If you go after a room now it's "men only".' I said, 'I've been after a room today—five pound a week for a basement room and three months' rent in advance. That's £55 before you could sleep in the bed! And there's nothing to see. There's only just a blinking old iron bedstead and a table and a chair and a wardrobe and a tiny little wooden dressing-table—things what you'd put on the dustheap. That's five pound a week! Then,' I said, 'I phoned after another one. That was £4.50 and three months' rent in advance. I offered him two weeks' rent and he wouldn't accept it. He said, "No, I want three months' rent in advance and a week's rent on top." '

She thought I was telling her lies. She said, 'You're a liar.' 'Oh well,' I said, 'if I'm a liar, I'm a liar.' I said, 'Just the same, Ann, I've got nothing to thank *you* for! From the time that you married my son what have you give to me? Nothing! Hardly ever a cup of tea even. *That's* too much trouble when I come down here.' I said, 'And I kept you in my flat for two and a half years when you got married,' I said, 'and what did you do in my flat? Bugger all. I had to go to work from eight till seven, then come home and do all the cooking, climb seven flights of stairs to feed *you*.' I said, 'I know you was having a baby and all that, but just the same you could have done something. You sat on your backside!' She said, 'What did you expect me to do— clean the flat all out!' I said, 'Well, Ann, yes. I had to go to work when I was pregnant,' I said, 'right until I was nine months.

When I had Michael,' I said, '*I* had no one to help *me*!' I said. 'I went to the hospital all on my own. When I was taken bad I asked Basit to make me a cup of tea. He said, "Get up and make it yourself!" Then he went out. When the water broke I had to run out and get the ambulance myself. Otherwise the baby might have been born indoors with no one in there, only myself. How about that? I had to help myself,' I said. 'You didn't have to do that, did you? You had all the sympathy in the world, didn't you? I rung for the ambulance for you five times. Four false alarms at two o'clock in the morning. Then come the final one at three o'clock in the morning. Who fetched the ambulance? Me, wasn't it? Nobody else. And now you're sitting and telling me that I'm lazy when I waited on you hand and foot!' I said, 'You had nothing to grumble about, Ann,' I said. 'Food and everything for a pound a week when the rent was £4–10! You've got a lot to talk about! Look at your own self! When your sisters come up here, what do they get? They get the best of everything—egg, chips and beans and bacon, the lot, and coffee and all, and bread and butter. "Do you want any more?"' 'Well that's my sisters!' 'Oh well then, I'm rubbish then, ain't I?' 'Yes,' she said, 'You are rubbish!' She said, 'I'm ashamed of you. I don't own you as my mother-in-law for living in the Salvation Army Hostel. When my sister met you that time in Commercial Road she thought you was a tramp!' I said to her, 'Would *you* be looking like a tramp if you'd been in the pouring rain?! I'd done someone a good turn! More than what you would have done! I saw a girl that looked very desperate in the Oxfam shop and I looked after her children,' I said, 'while she went to the Whitechapel Ladies Toilet to put on a new dress, and when she come back it was pouring with rain,' I said, 'and I took my coat off and wrapped it round her two children to keep them warm and we had to walk from Vallance Road right to Hackney Road Children's Hospital to see her little baby there who was very ill and on the danger list! And I looked for them children four or five hours while she was gone because after she'd fed the baby the Welfare Lady wanted to see her because she was getting a new flat!' So Ann said, 'I couldn't care less. The idiotic things that you would do I wouldn't do.' I said, 'My inside is different. I was brought up the hard way. And don't forget,' I said, 'I've helped Michael right from the time that he was born. His father never bought him no clothes. Only my money bought him clothes.' She said, 'I'm not interested. What you and your husband done is your affair, and what I do and Michael that's my business, nothing to do with you. If I want to give you a cup of tea, I give you a cup of tea. If I don't want to give you a cup of tea, I don't. I don't have to because I couldn't care less.' 'Well,' I said, 'I'm lucky to get a cup of tea. More often than not,' I said, 'I refuse because there's always a big argument. "Who's going to make it? Oh, Jane, are you going to make Nannie's tea?" "No, I want to watch the telly." "Ruth?" "No, I want to watch the telly." So in the end I've never bothered to have a tea, have I? And you can't deny that, can you?' She didn't like that. 'But,' I said, 'when your sisters come up, what do they get? They get the best of everything.' 'Oh well, that's my own flesh and blood.' I turned round and I said to her, 'You ought to be ashamed of yourself to talk to me like that after what I done for you when you got married to Michael!' She said, 'I married your son. What do you expect me to do? Get down and kiss your feet and give you five pound in the hand? I won't give you nothing.' I said, 'All the years you married him have you *ever* given me anything?' I said, 'No, never! I've got nothing to say thank you for for all the years you married him and all the time that you went with him.' I said, 'I waited on you hand and foot. Egg and chips. Bread and butter. Cups of tea. Biscuits and cake.' All the time she was courting she used to come to the flat nearly every night and every *morning*! She used to be up there half past seven—cup of tea, buttered roll, toast. She wouldn't go to work without him! 'Yes,' I said, 'and all your friends come here and you wait on them hand and foot and give them this and give them that, and you give me nothing! I've got nothing to thank you for!' I said, 'You're too high and mighty!' I said. 'You think too much of yourself.' I said, 'How about your friend opposite when she comes here? "Come on, darling, and sit down!" and all that!! Michael comes home with blouses and you've sold them to your friends, but have you ever asked if I wanted to buy one? No. Never.' I said, 'When he got those six or seven blouses a pound each did you ask me? Oh no. You was going to ask your friends!'

Then I went out of the flat and she run after me, and Michael he run after her and caught her and he dragged her back. He said, 'If she'd have got hold of you, Mum, she would have killed you!' She was hysterical, screaming. And I was screaming and all. I said, 'I walked all the way from Hopetown Street to be treated like that!'

Then there was another row when I went there last week. When I knocked, Michael come to the door. He didn't really want to see me. He said, 'Oh Christ! What you?!' I said, 'I've only come to talk with you, love, that's all.' He said, 'I'm not interested.' 'Oh well, then,' I said, 'I'm wasting my time. But your friend's come back from Bangladesh, the one you used to meet in the restaurant in New Road.' 'I don't want to know any coloured people. They're rubbish to me. I don't want to know him. I don't want to see him. And don't you ever send him round my place,' he said, 'or let him know where I live!' I thought, 'I daren't go and tell him Michael doesn't want to know him. He wouldn't like that!' I said, 'All right. I won't come here. You don't want to know me. I've got no money but that's the way you get treated.' I said, 'I've got no mother to look forward to. I've got no father. I've never seen my sisters and my brother since we buried Mum in 1947. I've only got you and Derek, and Derek I've never seen for eight years. I think it's disgusting when you've got two boys,' I said, 'who treat me like this when you see what other boys do for their mother. Knowing what I've done for you since you was babies, it don't make sense to me. If you don't want to know me it's just too bad.'

When I come out I cried.

I don't think now he's going to help me with my flat after all. He promised me he'd help but I think he's changed his mind. I'll have to do it all on my own. 'When you get your flat,' he said, 'what you want to do, you do!' The Welfare Lady said, 'Mrs Ali, how does your son feel?' I said, 'He couldn't care less and yet him and his wife don't like the idea of me being in the Salvation Army and she thinks I'm too lazy to look for a place.' She said, 'I think she ought to be ashamed of herself. And I'd have thought *he* could have done something for you before now, your son. He couldn't think much of you, Mrs Ali, allowing you to stay in the Salvation Army after all them years, knowing that you was desperate. And letting you sit in Swanfield Street for six months till you saved the money to go and pay the electric bill—no wireless, no nothing. Oh,' she said, 'I wouldn't bother with a boy like that. Bigger fool for you to go and see him. I'd wipe the floor with him,' she said. 'Mrs Ali, do me a favour and forget about him.'

There's another thing happened that's come as a bit of a shock and all. Derek who took a house with his job, Michael told me he's give up the house and job and he's had a divorce because he found Sheila was mucking around with somebody else. Sheila's another one that didn't help at Laleham. She couldn't be bothered even cleaning her room out. Come a time when I happened to go into the room and I saw it was in a shocking state. I thought, 'Oh good God Almighty! Let's do this room out!' It was filthy! I cleaned the room out, fumigated it. I done all the windows. I put all lovely curtains to the windows. I done all the mantelpiece, the dressing-table, the chair, the table, everything. All lovely and clean. I changed the bed—all clean sheets and pillowcases, nice clean bedcover. Oh the room looked wonderful! Then I went round and picked up all the dirty things and took them to the washing machine and dried them and come back and pressed them and put them on the chair. And when she come back and saw what I'd done she never spoke to me for two weeks. I said to Derek, 'What's wrong with Sheila, Derek?' He said, 'It's because you went in the room, Mum, and done it. Don't touch our room from now on. Leave the room alone. Do me a favour.' I said, 'Is that the way you get treated then, Derek, for what I done? I thought that she'd have been only too pleased.' 'No,' he said. 'She was wild thinking that you went in and found the room and done it.' 'Well,' I said, 'I had to, Derek. Look at the state of the room!' He said, '*She* could have done it.' I said, 'Well she's had plenty of bloody time to do it, hasn't she? Don't make me bloody sick, Derek. She's only a young girl. No children. No nothing. And I'm working from eight till seven and I come home every night and cook your food for you and her to sit down and eat.' I said, 'That girl never gets up and makes a cup of tea!' I said, 'She goes to her mother's home, takes new blankets for her sisters—bedcovers, the lot. What the hell did she buy me for Christmas? Bugger all. Ten cigarettes—and she didn't buy those till Boxing Day when she made up her mind to go to the sweet shop! Come back, said, "Here you are, Mum. Here's ten cigarettes". I was numbed, thinking, "Christ! Looking after her for two and a half years—and ten cigarettes!!" Oh good God!'

And then they moved out, went to Stoke Newington. And when she began to put on a bit of weight the landlady said, 'Take a week's notice!' and they come crying back to me again. And I took them back. Pound a week for the two of them! All their food, breakfast, supper, bedlinen, gas, electric, everything till they went to Shepherdess Walk!

That's how children are. Once they get married you've had your chips. They don't want to know you. You're old, you see. They couldn't care less. Just like the Salvation Army. There's one woman in the hostel that's been in the Bancroft Road Hospital. Cor, love a duck, she looked lovely and fat! Wonderful she looked! Now she's going to rack and ruin. I don't know what this Salvation Army is coming to. She can't hardly walk. The woman's got no strength. She should be in an Old Ladies Home and be looked after properly. Give and take, for God's sake! No chocolates. No packets of biscuits. No bananas. Oh it's heart breaking, knowing that they have all that Pension Money in that office! Them pensioners, they've worked all their lives for this money. Old people want nourishment, not punishment.

Cor, good God Almighty, do you know what?, honest to God, I've gone out of that Salvation Army Hostel and I've seen these people that lay around and sleep out all night, I've gone out with ten cigarettes and if I meet them people I give them one each. I couldn't help it. It's my nature. People say, 'Beatty, why do you do this?' I say, 'I know what it is myself. I know what it is to want.'

Someone saw me with this old man, they said, '*I* wouldn't do it. I wouldn't have no interest if I went out with an old man like that.' I said, 'What you would do and what I would do is two different things. My heart is soft. If I thought anybody needed food and I had the money I'd buy it for them. If I had two shillings and someone needed a shilling I'd give it to them.' This old man, bless him, he couldn't thank me enough. He said, 'Oh you are so kind to me. I do appreciate this kindness.' The morning after I put him in this armchair I went round to the Maltese shop near the nuns' and got him a cup of tea and took it to him—he'd been out all night sitting in this big armchair. 'Here you are, Dad. Here's a cup of tea and a couple of cigarettes. And here you are, here's ten pence.' I said, 'Are you all right, Dad?' He said, 'I'm all right. Don't worry. But come back and see me again. I always look forward to you. You are so kind.'